T0190356

Computer Vision and Augmented Reality in iOS

OpenCV and ARKit Applications

Ahmed Fathi Bekhit

Apress®

Computer Vision and Augmented Reality in iOS: OpenCV and ARKit Applications

Ahmed Fathi Bekhit
Boca Raton, FL, USA

ISBN-13 (pbk): 978-1-4842-7461-3   ISBN-13 (electronic): 978-1-4842-7462-0
https://doi.org/10.1007/978-1-4842-7462-0

Managing Director, Apress Media LLC: Welmoed Spahr
Acquisitions Editor: Aaron Black
Development Editor: James Markham
Coordinating Editor: Jessica Vakili

Distributed to the book trade worldwide by Springer Science+Business Media New York, 233 Spring Street, 6th Floor, New York, NY 10013. Phone 1-800-SPRINGER, fax (201) 348-4505, e-mail orders-ny@springer-sbm.com, or visit www.springeronline.com. Apress Media, LLC is a California LLC and the sole member (owner) is Springer Science + Business Media Finance Inc (SSBM Finance Inc). SSBM Finance Inc is a **Delaware** corporation.

For information on translations, please e-mail booktranslations@springernature.com; for reprint, paperback, or audio rights, please e-mail bookpermissions@springernature.com.

Apress titles may be purchased in bulk for academic, corporate, or promotional use. eBook versions and licenses are also available for most titles. For more information, reference our Print and eBook Bulk Sales web page at http://www.apress.com/bulk-sales.

Any source code or other supplementary material referenced by the author in this book is available to readers on GitHub via the book's product page, located at www.apress.com/978-1-4842-7461-3. For more detailed information, please visit http://www.apress.com/source-code.

Printed on acid-free paper

*This book is dedicated to the memory of
Daniel Bakhtiyarov.*

Table of Contents

About the Author

Ahmed Fathi Bekhit is Cofounder and Chief Technology Officer at Magic Studio, a software company based in Boca Raton, Florida, that focuses on developing cutting-edge video processing and streaming technologies. In the early days of Ahmed's career in software engineering, he was awarded the Apple WWDC Scholarship three times in a row and was also titled "Apple's Whiz Kid" by *The Wall Street Journal* at the age of 15.

As of today, Ahmed has worked as a software engineer with a few startups for seven years, and he has been writing software for over a decade. He also regularly contributes to the open source community and has been known for creating ARVideoKit, an iOS framework that renders ARKit content to capture videos, GIFs, and live photos with Augmented Reality components. In addition to developing software, Ahmed has interest in writing educational material that is focused on software engineering to share his background and knowledge with others. For example, he contributed various articles on the tutorial site AppCoda. He also published educational material through Stanford University's Scholar Initiative. Additionally, over the past few years, Ahmed developed and published independent iOS applications that reached over five million users. Ahmed's engineering work has been notably integrated in Emmy-winning software and licensed to help with the COVID vaccine manufacturing pipeline.

About the Technical Reviewer

 **Massimo Nardone** has more than 22 years of experience in security, web/mobile development, and cloud and IT architecture. His true IT passions are security and Android.

He has been programming and teaching how to program with Android, Perl, PHP, Java, VB, Python, C/C++, and MySQL for more than 20 years.

He holds a Master of Science degree in computing science from the University of Salerno, Italy.

He has worked as a project manager, software engineer, research engineer, chief security architect, information security manager, PCI/SCADA auditor, and senior lead IT security/cloud/SCADA architect for many years.

Acknowledgments

I would like to acknowledge the extraordinary support I have received from family and friends throughout the journey of writing this book; I am extremely fortunate and grateful to have such an amazing support system around me. Thank you, David Parshenkov, Fathi Bekhit, Mohamed Bekhit, Hazem Abdeltawab, Youssef Gamal, Ahmed Abdulkareem, Seif Hediya, and Amr Aly, for all the love and support you have given me that encouraged me throughout this journey. I love you all.

This book is a reality today thanks to Aaron Black, Senior Acquisitions Editor at Apress, for believing in me; Jessica Vakili, Coordinating Editor at Apress, for the continual support and feedback; Akanksha Devkar, Deep Learning Engineer, for the amazing feedback to make this book comprehensive; and Affan Abbas, Deep Learning Researcher, for the brilliant input and feedback on state-of-the-art computer vision technologies used in academia today.

Last but not least, thank you, Leo, for being there for me in the late nights I spent writing this book. I could not have done it without you.

CHAPTER 1

Introduction to Computer Vision

This chapter will focus on what computer vision is, why we need it, the evolution of the technology, its different applications, and how it is used in Augmented Reality.

What Is Computer Vision?

Vision is the ability to analyze and interpret scenes and objects of interest. Human vision has been studied for hundreds of years to understand how the visual process works. The human visual process is one of the most complex processes to understand. In fact, to this day, vision scientists have not yet found a complete answer to how the visual process works. However, vision scientists' discoveries on how the human visual process begins and a little beyond that inspired computer scientists to develop what we know today as Computer Vision. Vision researchers and scientists describe that the visual process begins with the eyes processing signals of light and converting them into scenes and images for the brain's visual cortex to analyze and interpret. A breakthrough in vision research in the 1950s discovered that the visual process begins by detecting the simple structures and edges of an image to help build up a more detailed interpretation as the visual information becomes more complex. The

© Ahmed Fathi Bekhit 2022
A. F. Bekhit, *Computer Vision and Augmented Reality in iOS*,
https://doi.org/10.1007/978-1-4842-7462-0_1

breakthrough vision research inspired computer scientists to develop the preprocessing Computer Vision algorithms we use today to initiate every computer vision task. Compared to a typical computer today, the human brain computing speed is significantly slower than a computer's computing speed, yet the human brain performs vision tasks much faster and significantly better than any computer. Hence, researchers' inspiration to develop Computer Vision algorithms has always been the evolution of vision in nature.

Computer Vision is the field of studying and developing technology that enables computers to process, analyze, and interpret digital images. Today, Computer Vision applications can be found in several industries, such as industrial robots, medical imaging, surveillance, and many more. All these applications have one principal mission, and it is processing, analyzing, and interpreting the contents of digital images to perform a task relevant to an industry's needs, which will be referred to as a vision task in the rest of this book. A vision task is any kind of task that requires processing, analyzing, or interpreting the contents of digital images and videos. For reference, a video is a sequence of digital images, typically consisting of 30–60 digital images per second, also referred to as frames.

Computers display digital images very often. When a digital image is given to a computer as an input, the computer reads it as a two-dimensional array of pixels; it can also be defined as a two-dimensional matrix. An image matrix consists of M columns and N rows. The size of an image in pixels can be determined by finding the product of M *columns* and N *rows* ($M \times N$), where M is the width and N is the height of the image. A pixel position is identified by its x and y coordinates (x, y) in the matrix. The coordinate system in computer graphics and digital images is slightly different from a typical Cartesian coordinate system; the point of origin ($0, 0$) in a digital image begins from the top-left corner of the image. Therefore, x is increasing from left to right, and y is increasing from top to bottom (see Figure 1-1).

Figure 1-1. *Digital Image Coordinate System*

In a grayscale digital image, a pixel value can be represented in various formats; however, the most common format used is an 8-bit (1-byte) unsigned integer ranging from 0 to 255 where 0 is black and 255 is white. Any value between 0 and 255 defines a different shade of gray (see Figure 1-2).

Magnified 16x16 Grayscale Image   **The Image Matrix**

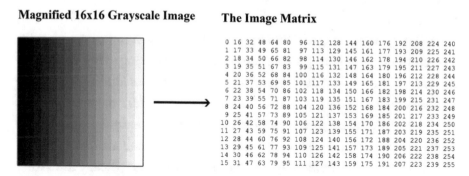

Figure 1-2. *Grayscale Image Converted to a Matrix*

Figure 1-2 demonstrates a 16 × 16 grayscale image converted to pixel values that are represented in 8-bit unsigned integers.

In a color digital image, a pixel value must be specified in three colors – red, green, and blue – which represents an RGB color space. Thus, the pixel value is represented as a vector of three numbers where each number ranges from 0 to 255. As the number increases, the *brightness* of each color increases, also referred to as *color intensity*. For example, if a given pixel

3

value is (255, 255, 255), this means the red, green, and blue intensities (or brightness) are set to their highest value, which defines a *white* pixel (see Figure 1-3).

Red Intensity	0	255	255	0	0
Green Intensity	0	255	0	255	0
Blue Intensity	0	255	0	0	255

Figure 1-3. RGB Color Space and Color Intensity Example

In Figure 1-3 you can see how the color intensity can affect the final resulting color. The higher the color intensity, the brighter the resulting color.

Although rendering a digital image appears to be a computer-friendly task, computer vision requires more complex processing to interpret, analyze, or manipulate the contents of a digital image. Computer Vision consists of two core applications: **manipulating digital images** and **processing digital images** to perform vision tasks. Manipulating digital images includes image enhancement, restoration, reconstruction, and compression. Image enhancement and restoration are typically used to improve the quality of distorted images. Reconstruction of images takes advantage of a set of two-dimensional images from different angles to reconstruct a three-dimensional image. However, some implementations that use deep learning attempt to reconstruct a three-dimensional image from a single two-dimensional image. Image compression is used to convert images into a more efficient representation to minimize storage usage. Processing digital images, on the other hand, may use some image manipulation techniques to perform vision tasks that match, describe, or recognize the contents of an image. The process of matching and describing contents of an image mainly depends on segmenting images into smaller parts and comparing the segmented parts to other template images and measuring the relationships between the segmented parts and the template images (see Figure 1-4).

Image Credits: Racool_studio/Freepik.com

Figure 1-4. *Template Matching Abstract Example*

Figure 1-4 demonstrates a sample result of a template matching algorithm.

An Overview on How Computer Vision Works

In order for a computer to perform a vision task, such as face detection, it requires performing several smaller tasks to reach the target task. For example, in order to perform a vision task, a computer typically has to perform various digital image preprocessing techniques, such as grayscale manipulation, edge enhancement and detection, noise removal, image restoration, interpolation, and image segmentation. Image preprocessing is the first stage in every vision task, and it plays a significant role to have a successful outcome. The purpose of preprocessing is extracting the valuable parts in a given image and getting rid of unwanted distortions.

The valuable parts help in developing useful descriptions of pixels, shapes, and surfaces in a given image. As we mentioned earlier, a pixel value is defined by either a 1-byte integer (when it is in a grayscale image) or a vector of integers representing an RGB color space (when it is in a color image); and each pixel value has a different intensity level representing the brightness of the color. The changes of intensity in a given image provide clues about the structure of shapes and surfaces in the image.

In the preprocessing stage, we try to extract this information without any knowledge of the contents of an image using techniques, such as noise removal, edge enhancement, and image segmentation. Noise removal is the process of smoothing an image to reduce and eliminate unwanted noise/distortion. However, sometimes noise removal techniques end up blurring the image; in this case, edge enhancement techniques come in handy. Edge enhancement helps with improving the sharpness of the edges in an image by increasing the intensity level difference between the boundaries of two regions (see Figure 1-5).

Figure 1-5. *Edge Enhancement/Detection Example*

The image on the left is the original image. The image on the right is the resulting image after applying an edge enhancement technique. As you may have noticed, the right image appears to "outline" the edges of the dog, which can be used in various vision tasks, such as image classification.

Image segmentation is the process of separating an image into smaller parts called segments. Segments are used to process the parts of an image separately, because in many cases an image has more than just one unique object or feature that can help identify the contents of the image. Image segmentation is considered an intermediate step between preprocessing and processing an image for object detection or segment classification (see Figure 1-6).

Figure 1-6. *Abstract Computer Vision Pipeline*

After preprocessing a digital image, the processing steps begin, and in many cases, it may involve techniques such as feature extraction, texture analysis, and pattern recognition. Depending on each vision task, you would pick the more relevant technique to perform the task. For example, to perform an image classification task, you would use a feature extraction technique to extract unique features in the segments of a given image. The segments of an image are extracted during the image segmentation process. Once the unique features are extracted from the image segments, they are used to find a distinct pattern matching predefined or labeled image segments; a labeled image segment is a piece of an image that is manually defined under human supervision (Figure 1-7).

Figure 1-7. *Labeled Image Segments Example*

The process of finding an exact match to a labeled segment is called feature matching; and the process of finding a distinct pattern is called pattern recognition. Figure 1-6 demonstrates an abstract Computer Vision pipeline and what a given image has to typically go through when a computer is performing a vision task. Further details on different image processing techniques will be covered throughout the book.

Why Do We Need Computer Vision?

Since the Internet has been accessible to billions of users around the world, it has enabled many to capture, produce, and publish media-rich content, such as images, videos, and animated images (also known as GIFs). User-generated content defines the Internet we know today, and the amount of media-rich content published per day is rapidly increasing. Today, YouTube publishers alone contribute 300 hours of video per minute; that is 3 million hours of video per week. There is no human who can handle watching this much video at this rate. YouTube and many similar companies that allow user-generated content on their platforms are challenged to index, classify, and categorize billions of user-generated images and videos to provide their viewers the most relevant content they would watch. The categorization of all this content cannot be properly handled by a typical software; most of the existing approaches depend on the publishers' text input, such as video title, description, keywords, etc. However, in many cases, the publisher's text input can be irrelevant; and their content may contain inappropriate or violent scenes that should not be displayed to certain age groups, or many viewers would want to opt out of viewing such content. The only technology that would enable large-scale image and video indexing, classification, and categorization is Computer Vision. Computer Vision is needed by companies, such as

YouTube, to index and categorize the massive amount of media-rich content. In addition to categorizing images and videos, computer vision can be used to

-   Provide a visual description of images and videos to the visually impaired users and customers.

-   Filter inappropriate content to certain age groups.

-   Warn viewers of the type of scenes and content included in an image or a video.

-   Detect manipulated images and videos that may cause harm to the viewers or persons in the manipulated content.

In addition to the Internet-related problems Computer Vision can solve, there are many other problems across various industries that need computer vision technology to be solved. Now, you can find computer vision technology integrated in many things we interact with on a daily basis, such as cashier systems, surveillance systems, biometric scanners, medical equipment, transportation, and many more.

-   Cashier systems integrate computer vision technology to enable self-checkout kiosks.

-   Surveillance systems use image and video enhancement algorithms to detect and analyze the contents of surveillance images and videos.

-   Biometric scanners use edge detection and enhancement techniques to collect and analyze biometric information (i.e. fingerprints, facial features, eye features... etc).

-   Medical equipment takes advantage of various computer vision techniques, such as image reconstruction and restoration to retrieve useful information from medical devices and scanners.

The list can go on for pages demonstrating all the different applications of computer vision. In fact, the need of computer vision technology has been only increasing over the past decade. Top companies are adopting the technology in their products, and new companies are starting to provide computer vision–powered products. The impact of computer vision technology is limitless, and it will be adopted by more industries and organizations around the world over the next couple years. You may have already seen the initial iterations of the future of computer vision applications, such as self-driving vehicles, autonomous manufacturing, and education via Augmented Reality.

In 2019, companies' demand on Augmented Reality, Virtual Reality, and Computer Vision engineers has increased by 1500% (State of Software Engineers, Hired.com). Computer Vision will have a great impact on society in the following years and will require more contributors to the technology, which this book will intend to do by enabling software engineers and persons with interest in computer vision to be part of the development of this revolutionary technology.

The Evolution of Computer Vision

In 1959, a neurophysiology research conducted a couple experiments on a cat's visual system. The experiments placed electrodes in the main visual cortex of a cat's brain, and the researchers observed the neural response of the visual cortex as they presented various images to the cat (Figure 1-8).

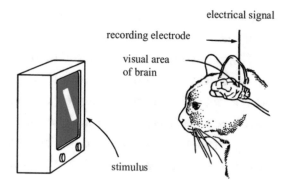

Figure 1-8. *Hubel and Wiesel's Experiment*

As the experiments went on, the researchers noticed a pattern in the cat's neural response when presented with a new image. The research concluded that there are simple and complex neurons in the visual cortex. And the visual process begins by detecting the simple structures and edges of an image to help build up a more detailed interpretation. As the visual information becomes more complex, the visual cortex depends on the complex neurons to interpret the remaining details of an image. This research later became to be one of the most influential research in the field of Computer Vision. It inspired Computer Vision researchers to achieve what is known today as image preprocessing.

In July of 1966, Seymour Papert, a professor at the Artificial Intelligence Lab at Massachusetts Institute of Technology (MIT), initiated "The Summer Vision Project." The project was assigned to undergraduate MIT students to develop pattern recognition technology in an attempt to enable machines to see. The project was a very optimistic plan to develop what we know today as Computer Vision in one summer. There were various attempts in the 1960s to develop a computer visual system; however, researchers eventually came to realize that such a project would require years, if not decades, to achieve. And here we are, 50 years later, and Computer Vision is still in the research and development phases.

Since the 1960s, Computer Vision has evolved to the technology we see in many applications today. One of the pioneering research in computer vision was in the 1970s, where the research focused on object recognition. The initial iteration of object recognition was abstract and simple to prove the concept of object recognition. The implementation used the line joints of simple objects, such as cylinders and cubes, to identify them. In the following decades, researchers and engineers developed the core techniques of traditional computer vision, which consists of two principal stages:

1. Image preprocessing

2. Image processing

The image preprocessing stage focuses on enhancing image colors and edges to help in detecting simple structures in a given image. The processing stage uses the preprocessed image to perform one or more of the following processing techniques:

– Image compression

– Image enhancement

– Image restoration and reconstruction

– Pattern matching and recognition

Although traditional image processing techniques such as the ones listed previously have been used for decades since their development, there have been a few problems these techniques alone would not solve, such as recognizing objects in a significantly unusual or unexpected context, such as handwritten words, digits, and images of objects captured from an unusual angle (Figure 1-9).

Normal Image of a Dog   Unusual Image of a Dog

Figure 1-9. *Normal vs. Unusual Image of an Object*

Consequently, in the 1980s, various groundbreaking research were published. The research suggested using an artificial network of simple and complex "neurons" that could recognize certain patterns. This artificial network is today referred to as an Artificial Neural Network (ANN). A Neural Network is a computing model that is designed to recognize patterns in a given set of labeled data (labeled images in this case). The network uses the given images to recognize a pattern and predict the results of each image. Once the network predicts the results of an image, it compares its prediction to the labels assigned to the image. The comparison stage enables the network to "learn" from the errors in its initial process, and then it performs the same process multiple times until the network provides more accurate results. Neural Networks often required lots of labeled data to provide significantly good results. Hence, in the early days, a Neural Network was not used to its full potential due to the lack of data.

In the early 2010s, a group of Computer Vision researchers initiated a large-scale image dataset with millions of images and over 20,000 categories, called ImageNet. ImageNet was inspired by the need of more data in the Computer Vision field. And it enabled the development of state-of-the-art Neural Network Models that had a great influence on the advanced computer vision applications seen today. Neural Networks and their variations are considered part of the field of Deep Learning, which is a subset of Machine Learning. Therefore, when Neural Networks are used to perform vision tasks, I will be referring to it as Deep Learning–based Computer Vision.

Traditional vs. Deep Learning–Based Computer Vision

Traditional Computer Vision has existed ever since the computer vision field began. Traditional Computer Vision techniques have been used for decades to efficiently perform vision tasks. The traditional techniques helped develop many algorithms that are commonly used today, such as Scale-Invariant Feature Transform (SIFT) and Speeded-Up Robust Features (SURF). Algorithms like SIFT and SURF have been a fundamental part of developing today's Augmented Reality technology due to their efficient performance and accurate results. However, in some cases, traditional computer vision techniques are not the best choice due to the lack of accuracy. In these cases, the best option is typically using a deep learning–based technique. Deep learning is used in several ways to perform complex vision tasks, such as image classification. Deep learning–based approaches typically outperform traditional approaches when it comes to image classification. Image classification is the process of classifying the contents of an image between separate categories. For example, one of the most popular image classification problems is classifying images of cats and dogs. When a software is presented with an image of a cat, it should classify it as a cat with high accuracy. Before deep learning, this task was nearly impossible to achieve; however, deep learning pushed the limits of what is possible to achieve in Computer Vision and successfully enabled a computer to differentiate between a cat and a dog with high accuracy. This would have not been possible without extremely fast computers and datasets of millions of cat and dog images. You may wonder why deep learning would require fast computers and a huge amount of data. Well, the answer lies behind what deep learning is and how it really works. Deep learning is a subset of machine learning that is largely established on Artificial Neural Networks (ANNs), a computing model inspired by how the human brain operates. Similar to the human brain, an Artificial Neural Network consists of several computing "neurons." An artificial neuron in a Neural Network performs a simple computing operation that communicates with other connected neurons in the network to make a decision. Each neuron connection to another neuron has a certain strength. The strengths of connections between neurons are called weights (see Figure 1-10).

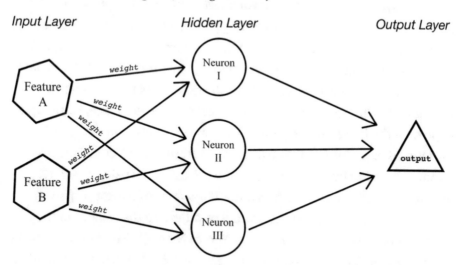

Figure 1-10. *Feedforward Artificial Neural Network Model*

Figure 1-10 is demonstrating a simple Neural Network consisting of three layers—(1) Input Layer, (2) Hidden Layer, (3) Output Layer:

1. The Input Layer consists of multiple inputs where each input represents a unique feature about the given dataset.

2. The Hidden Layer is a set of neurons that calculates and processes in a certain way depending on the weight value.

3. The Output Layer is the last layer in a Neural Network that receives the final results from the previous Hidden Layer.

A set of neurons represents a Neural Network Hidden Layer, and a typical deep learning algorithm consists of multiple Neural Network Hidden Layers. ANNs consist of two phases, the learning phase and the performing phase. During the learning phase, a Neural Network takes advantage of a labeled dataset to "learn" the correlation between the data and their description (also known as labels). In our case, a labeled dataset would consist of a set of images with a description of the contents of each image. When a Neural Network is given a labeled image, it attempts to process the image in the Hidden Layers and return a prediction of the label as an output. Once an output is returned, the Neural Network "grades" its result by comparing it to the original label using a variety of functions called objective functions. If the grade does not surpass a certain threshold, it will "learn" from it by adjusting the weights of the connections between neurons in the Neural Network. The Neural Network continues learning by presenting the same input to itself, and the weights of the network are adjusted as it learns. This process repeats multiple times until the Neural Network's "grade" surpasses the required threshold. The process of "learning" and adjusting weights is called Backward

Propagation of Errors, also known as Backpropagation. To recap, here is a simple ordered list of the steps a typical Artificial Neural Network goes through to "learn" something new:

1. Receives labeled input

2. Attempts to predict the input's label

3. Returns the predicted label as an output

4. Compares the predicted label to the actual label

5. Grades the results

6. Adjusts the strengths of connections between neurons, also known as weights

7. Repeats the process until the final grade surpasses the threshold

Computer Vision in Augmented Reality

Augmented Reality (AR) is the technology that augments or displays digital objects in the physical world through a camera live feed. In order to display digital objects in the physical world, we would need to understand and detect objects of the physical world in real time. In some cases, the objects can be a specific template. In other cases, it can be a horizontal surface, such as a desk and a floor, or it can be a vertical surface, such as a wall and a door. To be able to detect objects and surfaces, we would need to use Computer Vision techniques to display digital objects in the physical world. There are three main types of Augmented Reality: Marker-Based, Marker-Less, and Geolocation Augmented Reality. Marker-Based AR requires a certain predefined template to display digital objects on. For example, a page in a book or a magazine can have a special icon so when a camera detects that icon it would display a digital object mapped on the icon or the page (Figure 1-11).

Marker-Based AR   **Marker-Less AR**

Figure 1-11. *Marker-Based vs. Marker-Less AR*

Unlike Marker-Based AR, Marker-Less AR does not require any special predefined templates to display digital objects. Instead, it can place digital objects on any horizontal or vertical surfaces using various Computer Vision techniques. Geolocation AR, in many cases, depends on either Marker-Based or Marker-Less AR and integrates location sensor technologies to display digital objects in the physical world based on visual and location data.

Augmented Reality today is mostly accessible through mobile devices, smartphones to be more specific. Although there have been various attempts to integrate immersive AR experiences by developing custom hardware and devices, such as Microsoft's HoloLens, Magic Leap Glasses, and Google Glasses, it is too early for consumers to adapt to using new and unfamiliar hardware. Therefore, smartphones were the perfect tool to introduce consumers to AR. In the early days of mobile AR, using markers, such as a QR code or a template image, was the main way to augment digital objects in the physical world. To achieve that, techniques such as pattern recognition and pose estimation were required. Pattern recognition is a technique that depends on a predefined set of data describing features to find and analyze in a given image. Pose estimation uses the detected pattern to simulate a three-dimensional pose based on the camera angle (see Figure 1-12); this technique is used to enable seeing a three-dimensional object from all angles based on the camera's point of view.

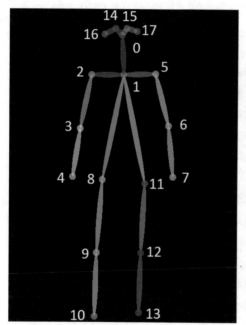

Figure 1-12. *Body Pose Estimation*

Marker-Based AR allowed any user with access to a smartphone to interact and use the technology; however, the requirement of having a physical marker was not scalable nor practical for daily use. Therefore Marker-Less AR had more potential due to its ease of use and accessibility. In the early days of Marker-Less AR development, dual cameras were required to have a reconstruction of the physical world.

Summary

In this chapter, we read about the history of Computer Vision. Grayscale and color images were compared. We also studied why we need Computer Vision and its evaluation. We also saw a simplified architecture of a Feedforward Artificial Neural Network. Finally, we looked at Augmented Reality.

To conclude, computer vision is a field of Artificial Intelligence (AI) that enables computers and systems to derive meaningful information from digital images, videos, and other visual inputs and take actions or make recommendations based on that information. If AI enables computers to think, computer vision enables them to see, observe, and understand.

Computer vision works much the same as human vision, except humans have a head start. Human sight has the advantage of lifetimes of context to train how to tell objects apart, how far away they are, whether they are moving, and whether there is something wrong in an image.

In the next chapter, we'll take a look at Augmented Reality and different types of Augmented Reality.

CHAPTER 2

Introduction to Augmented Reality

This chapter will focus on what Augmented Reality is, the evolution of the technology, and its different applications.

What Is Augmented Reality?

Over the decades, humans have always used some sort of technology to visualize data, tell stories, educate students, and even be entertained. Data visualization has been essential for many organizations and individuals to better understand information and make decisions. Storytelling plays an important role in getting an audience engaged in an activity. Education is critical to enable today's students to form their future. Forms of entertainment can be video games, sports, and concerts. All these are examples of activities that can be much more interactive by augmenting digital objects in the physical world and enabling consumers to interact with them. To successfully augment digital objects in the physical world, we would have to project light into custom shapes and display it on physical objects. However, this approach would require additional hardware that is not commonly used by most consumers, such as screen projectors and holographic projectors. The fact that additional hardware is needed to "augment" digital objects in the physical world made the technology less

© Ahmed Fathi Bekhit 2022
A. F. Bekhit, *Computer Vision and Augmented Reality in iOS*,
https://doi.org/10.1007/978-1-4842-7462-0_2

accessible and hardly scalable due to the high price tag of the hardware needed. As the development of computer vision arose, more researchers and engineers worked together to develop various techniques to augment digital objects in the physical world and enable new ways to interact with computers, to develop what we know today as Augmented Reality.

Augmented Reality is the field of developing interactive user experiences by reconstructing and displaying interactive digital objects in the physical world. In the process of developing Augmented Reality technology and applications, we are required to take in consideration three core concepts:

1. Physical world reconstruction and mapping techniques

2. Digital object projection techniques

3. New human-computer interaction guidelines

One of the early approaches to augment and interact with digital objects in the physical world was a project developed by a computer researcher, Myron Krueger, who used a camera's live visual data and projected a computer interface to interact with the digital computer components in the physical world (Figure 2-1).

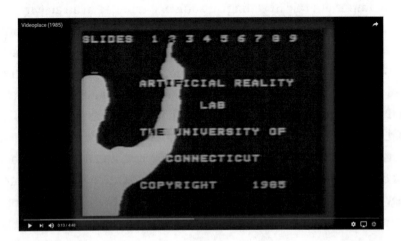

Figure 2-1. *Videoplace – Beginning of AR*

Many other approaches also depended on a camera's live visual data for scene understanding; but the projection of the digital components was always changing. Some attempts created headsets and glasses that would project the digital components on a small screen that was wearable. And others would stream the camera's live visual data to a computer screen and interact with the digital components through the screen. As computer vision technology evolved and camera devices with a live feed on a portable screen became more popular and accessible to consumers, the development of the Augmented Reality technology that we are familiar with today began. In addition to developing computer vision and digital object projection techniques to achieve Augmented Reality, making Augmented Reality human-friendly and easy to use is crucial to enable the full potential of the technology. Computer vision, hardware, and human-computer interaction researchers and engineers have been working together over the years to create the ultimate Augmented Reality experience, which led to developing the most common form of Augmented Reality seen today in mobile phones.

Today, smartphones, such as iOS and Android devices, are the main devices that enable users to experience Augmented Reality, given that the majority of smartphones have powerful cameras, sensors, and geolocation hardware. By making use of information provided by the hardware found in smartphones, we can provide an immersive and entertaining experience to the users through Augmented Reality. The hardware pieces in a smartphone that provide sufficient information to achieve Augmented Reality are single-lens or multi-lens cameras, accelerometers, gyroscopes, magnetometers, and geolocation sensors (Figure 2-2).

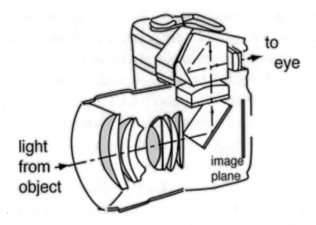

Figure 2-2. *Single-Lens Camera*

Single-lens cameras provide visual data of a scene from one angle, which helps in detecting and tracking simple features of a surface in a scene. Multi-lens cameras, on the other hand, provide visual data from two different angles, which helps in detecting and tracking the depth in a scene, and depth tracking enables a more accurate real-world distance measuring. Accelerometers, gyroscopes, and magnetometers are all part of a unit called Inertial Measurement Unit (IMU), which enables measuring a device's acceleration and estimating its velocity, distance, orientation, and gravitational force. Geolocation sensors provide information about the device's location and geographic coordinates, which enables augmenting and "pinning" digital objects in location-specific areas (Figure 2-3).

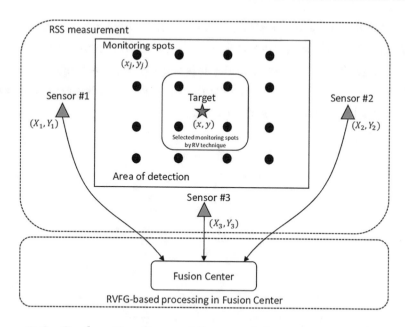

Figure 2-3. *Geolocation Sensor Measurement*

As mentioned previously, there are three core concepts we need to consider when developing Augmented Reality technology, and the first concept is physical world reconstruction and mapping, also referred to as scene reconstruction. Scene reconstruction is a computer vision task whose core objective is to reconstruct video frames into a three-dimensional scene. This vision task is essential to enable placing digital objects in a specific part of a room and identify an object's position in the physical world using a certain coordinate value retrieved from the reconstructed three-dimensional scene.

To perform this vision task, we would need to retrieve video frames from either a single-lens or a multi-lens camera. Video frames retrieved from a single-lens camera will make it more difficult to reconstruct the scene due to the lack of depth information; however, thanks to a computer vision technique known as structure from motion (SfM), scene reconstruction is possible to perform via a single-lens camera. SfM is a technique that uses an array of two-dimensional images to detect unique features in the array of images and reconstruct a three-dimensional scene (Figure 2-4). Unlike single-lens cameras, preforming scene reconstruction using images from multi-lens cameras is slightly less challenging since we can estimate depth from two or more images and reconstruct a three-dimensional scene using the depth data.

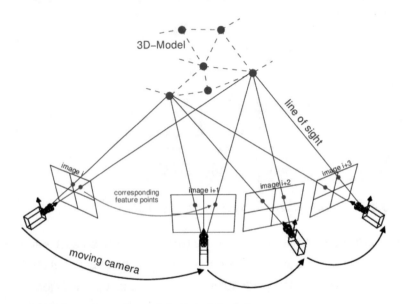

Figure 2-4. *Structure from Motion Model*

Although scene reconstruction using vision-only techniques could be sufficient in some cases, in many cases visual data coming from handheld mobile phones is distorted due to the excessive motion and unpredictable lighting conditions, leading to a large error margin and in some cases failing to achieve scene reconstruction. In this case, Inertial Measurement Units (IMUs) that can be found in most mobile phones today would be used alongside the visual data to result in the best scene reconstruction possible. Information retrieved from IMU devices, such as orientation and acceleration, is extremely helpful when the visual data is distorted or delayed for any reason since the IMU data is provided at a higher frequency than the visual data, which helps in detecting any small or significant changes in the motion and environment. Such IMU data is aligned with the visual data to compute the initial velocity and the physical coordinates of the device.

Using IMU data alongside the visual data from a camera has been a common approach used in the Computer Vision and Augmented Reality fields to perform scene reconstruction and other physical world measurement tasks. In fact, it is typically referred to as Visual-Inertial Odometry, VIO for short. VIO was initially developed for use in aerial robotics, such as drones, and vehicles to enable autonomous applications. As the technology evolved from only depending on multi-lens visual to single-lens visual data, its applications increased and eventually enabled Augmented Reality on smartphones. The Augmented Reality applications of VIO mainly revolve around "Marker-Less AR," which enables augmenting digital objects in the physical world without the requirement of a "marker." An AR marker is a uniquely identified object or image that is used to augment digital objects on; this can be a QR code, image in a book, or human/animal body parts, such as face, hands, and feet. To achieve Marker-Based Augmented Reality, various vision tasks are required, such as object pose estimation, annotation, and landmark detection.

Different Types of Augmented Reality

There are a few types of Augmented Reality that are commonly used today; that includes Marker-Based, Marker-Less, and Geolocation-Based Augmented Reality (AR). All three types' core objective is to augment digital objects in the physical world; however, the techniques used to achieve each type vary. Additionally, the applications of each type have different purposes. For example, Marker-Based AR requires previously defined image features that we can use to augment digital objects on. A commonly seen use case of this is Face Filters. AR Face Filters augment digital objects on or surrounding a detected face and track the face movements to change the digital objects' position accordingly (Figure 2-5).

Figure 2-5. *Face Detection and Landmark Estimation*

To achieve AR Face Filters, we would need to perform computer vision tasks, such as face detection and face landmark detection/tracking. Face detection is a process of segmenting and detecting a face from a given image. Face landmark detection is the process of detecting face features and tracking changes, such as eye blinking, mouth opening/closing, and facial expressions. By combining both information about the face in real time, we would be able to successfully augment digital objects on a face. In addition to using a detected face as a marker, there are other approaches that depend on various other markers, such as a simple QR code, a unique image, and custom physical objects (i.e., bottle, cup, hat, etc.). The processing techniques used to achieve other marker-based AR approaches are derived from the computer vision concepts of feature detection, tracking, and pose estimation. As we get closer to the implementation process at the end of this book, we will cover a more in-depth description of the algorithms used to achieve marker-based AR.

Marker-less AR is a robust technique that does not require any previous knowledge of an environment; however, it requires certain pieces of hardware to achieve it. In the early days of marker-less AR development, the type of hardware required to achieve marker-less AR was not commonly owned by consumers, such as stereo cameras and advanced IMU devices. As research and development of AR increased, we have seen various approaches to minimize the use of uncommon hardware and instead depend on hardware that is widely accessible to consumers, such as low-cost IMU devices and single-lens cameras, commonly found in smartphones today. In the previous section, we briefly covered how marker-less AR is achieved today in most mobile phones using Visual-Inertial Odometry techniques, which make use of information retrieved from both IMU devices and a camera to perform scene reconstruction alongside other computer vision tasks that would enable marker-less AR. Marker-less AR applications are limitless, and there is a lot of space for more creative and impactful applications. Today, marker-less AR can be used to measure physical objects and simulate an experience onto the physical world. These applications have had a great impact throughout many industries including education, design, tourism, and many more. To summarize, marker-less and marker-based AR are fundamentally the same but have completely different applications due to the restrictions each technology has. Despite the fact that these two AR approaches have extremely different applications, they can be used simultaneously to achieve a more complex Augmented Reality experience, which leads us to Geolocation-Based AR.

Geolocation-Based AR integrates both marker-less and marker-based AR with geographic location data to augment and "pin" digital objects in a specific geolocation coordinate (Figure 2-6).

Figure 2-6. *Geolocation-Based AR*

Summary

In this chapter, we discussed some basic concepts related to Augmented Reality. After that, different types of Augmented Reality were discussed.

AR can be defined as a system that incorporates three basic features: a combination of real and virtual worlds, real-time interaction, and accurate 3D registration of virtual and real objects.

The core components of any AR-based tool are the processor, sensors, input devices, and mainly the display. The display could be a smartphone, a handheld device, smart glasses, or a head-mounted display (HMD). The input devices are either cameras or web cams. Sensors include gyroscopes and accelerometers.

In the next chapter, we will take a look at image and video processing fundamentals in detail.

CHAPTER 3

Image and Video Processing Fundamentals

This chapter will focus on image and video processing fundamentals including required mathematics, standard algorithms, implementation options, and implementing a practical example into a C++ application.

Mathematics Overview

Mathematics has been the foundation of how computers work ever since the first computer was invented. In fact, one of the early applications of computers was in businesses that required computing/calculating complex mathematical problems in a short amount of time. As the computer hardware capabilities started improving over the decades, the amount of complex computation a computer can do in just a *second* has increased drastically, enabling computers to easily perform image and video processing, thus allowing computers to be used for high-speed and high-compute-power applications such as graphics processing and audio processing. In the previous chapters, we briefly went over how images are displayed, rendered, and processed. In this section, we will cover

© Ahmed Fathi Bekhit 2022
A. F. Bekhit, *Computer Vision and Augmented Reality in iOS*,
https://doi.org/10.1007/978-1-4842-7462-0_3

the mathematical fundamentals that enable today's image and video processing (also known as Computer Vision) and Artificial Intelligence technologies.

Although Computer Vision and Artificial Intelligence have a close relationship, their emphasis on mathematics differs slightly. The following radar plot summarizes the argument. In the following plot, you may see how Computer Vision incorporates different branches of mathematics compared to Artificial Intelligence/Deep Learning. Computer Vision leverages probability and statistics drastically more than Deep Learning (Figure 3-1).

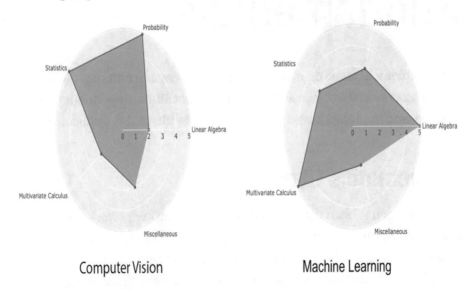

Figure 3-1. *Computer Vision vs. Machine Learning*

Although Computer Vision and Deep Learning have a lot in common, their main focus is extremely different. Our primary goal in Computer Vision is to investigate and analyze images or video, suggest recommendations, and validate them.

These seem to be the methods used to uncover hidden assumptions in data that are not visible at first glance. As a consequence, to compare and test hypothesis, we must rely solely on statistical and probability concepts (Figure 3-2). Both Computer Vision and Machine Learning emphasize on linear algebra principles since it is the starting point for all complicated systems. Multivariable calculus, on the other hand, is concerned with parameter analysis, which would be the driving factor behind all the Deep Neural Networks we will further discuss in this book.

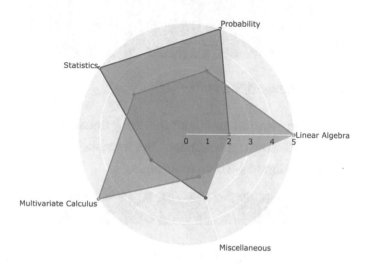

Figure 3-2. *Use of Math in Computer Vision*

Consider this. We prefer the data used in data mining techniques to be clean and prepared according to the methodology. If we want to work end to end (Computer Vision + Machine Learning), we should learn and explore the math fundamentals needed for Computer Vision and Artificial Intelligence applications.

In computer vision and machine learning, mathematics is not about analyzing data; it is about understanding what is going on, why it is occurring, and how we can experiment with different variables to get the outcome we desire. The graph below demonstrates the Rate of Change in a given variable; this is also known as rise over run, the slope formula, or sometimes referred to as the Gradient. Which allows us to understand the context of change from the given input.

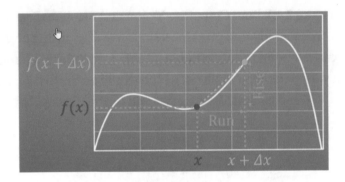

Graph for Rate of Change of Variable

Geometric interpretation and intuition of any linear equation is essential when processing a given image. The formula below is the standard representation of a Gradient formula:

$$\text{Gradient at } x \approx \frac{\text{Rise}}{\text{Run}} = \frac{f(x + \Delta x) - f(x)}{(x + \Delta x) - x} = \frac{f(x + \Delta x) - f(x)}{\Delta x}$$

Rate of Change of Variables (Differentiation)

This aids us in deciphering the interpretation of these perplexing statements.

Well, let's switch our emphasis to comprehending why we should have to learn these various branches of mathematics, as well as what would be a good source for learning them intuitively.

Image Processing Basics

At the moment, one of the hottest research areas is Deep Learning. Deep learning is a machine learning and Artificial Intelligence (AI) technique that mimics how people acquire certain types of knowledge. Deep learning algorithms are built in a hierarchy of increasing complexity and abstraction, unlike typical machine learning algorithms, which are linear. Deep learning as a field incorporates a range of academic disciplines, including computer science (graphics, algorithms, philosophy, structures, and architecture), mathematics (information retrieval, Machine Learning), engineering (robotics, voice, NLP, image processing), physics (optics), biology (neuroscience), and psychology (cognitive science), to name a few.

Because of its cross-domain mastery, many scientists agree that machine vision paves the way for Artificial General Intelligence because it represents a relative comprehension of visual environments and their contexts.

So What Is Computer Vision?

Definitions from the formal textbooks are given in the following:

- "The construction of explicit, meaningful descriptions of physical objects from images" (Ballard & Brown, 1982).

- "...computing properties of the 3D world from one or more digital images" (Trucco & Verri, 1998).

- "...to make useful decisions about real physical objects and scenes based on sensed images" (Sockman & Shapiro, 2001).

Why Computer Vision?

The most obvious response is that this area of research has an increasingly growing collection of practical applications. Here are only a few examples (Figure 3-3):

- Face recognition: To add filters and recognize you in images, Snapchat and Facebook use face detection algorithms.

- Picture retrieval: To locate appropriate images, Google Images uses content-based queries. The algorithms explore the content of the query image and return results depending on the content that is most closely related.

- Gaming and controls: Microsoft Kinect is a brilliant commercial device that uses stereo vision in gaming.

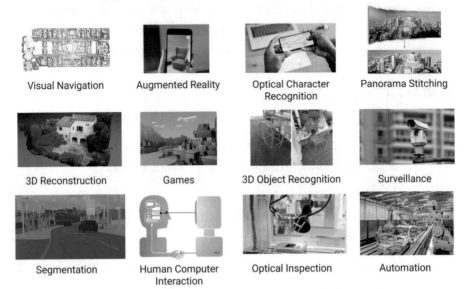

Figure 3-3. Applications of Computer Vision

- Surveillance cameras are common in public places and are used to track unusual activity.

- Fingerprint, iris, and face matching are some of the most popular biometric authentication techniques.

- Vision remains the primary source of knowledge for detecting road signals, lamps, and other visual features of smart vehicles.

Computer vision involves visual recognition such as image description, localization, and identification.

Standard Algorithms

The efficiency of these state-of-the-art visual recognition technologies has been vastly enhanced due to recent advancements in Neural Networks and deep learning approaches. This book is a great platform for learning about deep learning architectures and how they're used in cutting-edge machine vision science. In this book, we will go through the five most important computer vision strategies which are: Convolutional Neural Networks, AlexNet, Region-Based Convolutional Neural Network (R-CNN), and Fast R-CNN. Additionally, we will go through the main deep learning models and applications that each strategy can be used for.

Image Classification

Image classification's (Figure 3-4) goal is as follows: we're given a series of images that are all labeled with a single category, and we're asked to forecast these categories for a new set of test images, and we're asked to calculate the accuracy of our predictions. Viewpoint variance, size variation, intra-class variation, image deformation, image occlusion, lighting conditions, and context clutter are all problems that this activity presents.

Figure 3-4. *Image Classification*

How can we go about building an algorithm that can categorize images into various groups? Researchers in Computer Vision have devised a data-driven solution to this problem. They supply the computer with several examples of each image class and then create learning algorithms that look at these examples and learn about the visual appearance of each class, rather than attempting to determine what each of the image categories of interest looks like explicitly in code.

In other words, a training dataset of labeled images is first fed to the system to process and create a classification model accordingly. Here is a formalized version of the image classification pipeline:

- A training dataset containing N images, each labeled with one of K groups, is provided as input; where N is the total number of images in all groups and K is the number groups in the classification mode. A group represents the category the images belong to.

- Then we use this training package to teach a classifier how to classify the images.

- Finally, we measure the classifier's output by telling it to infer labels for a new series of images it has never seen before. The actual labels of these images would then be equivalent to the ones projected by the classifier.

Convolutional Neural Networks (CNNs) are the most commonly used image recognition architecture. When you feed the network images and the network classifies the data, this is a common use case for CNNs. A CNN typically begins with an input "scanner" that isn't designed to process all of the training data at once (Figure 3-5). When working with CNNs, you wouldn't want a layer with 10,000 nodes into which you input a 100 × 100–pixel file, for example. This would be extremely inefficient and not practical on a larger scale.

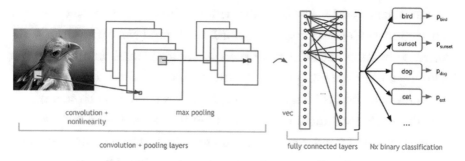

Figure 3-5. *Convolutional Neural Network*

Rather, you create a 10×10 scanning Input Layer into which you feed the image's first 10×10 pixels. After passing the data, move the scanner 1 pixel to the right to feed it the next 10×10 pixels. Sliding windows are the name for this process.

Convolutional layers, rather than regular layers, are used to process the input data. Each node is only concerned with cells in its immediate vicinity. These convolutional layers often appear to shrink as they get thicker, owing to quickly divisible input factors. They frequently have pooling layers in addition to convolutional layers. A popular pooling strategy is max pooling, in which we take, say, 2×2 pixels and move on to the pixel with the most of a certain attribute.

ImageNet, a dataset of nearly 1.2 million high-resolution training files, is used to train most image recognition techniques nowadays. Test images will be viewed with no initial annotation (i.e., no segmentation or labels), and algorithms will be required to create labeling showing which objects are present in the images. Leading computer vision groups from Oxford, INRIA, and XRCE tested some of the better current computer vision approaches on this dataset. Typically, computer vision solutions use multistage pipelines that are hand-tuned by tuning a few parameters in the early stages.

Alex Krizhevsky (NIPS 2012), the winner of the first ImageNet competition, built a very deep Convolutional Neural Net of the kind pioneered by Yann LeCun. It had seven secret layers in its architecture, not including any max pooling layers (Figure 3-6). The first two layers were convolutional, and the last layers were globally related. In each secret plate, the activation functions were linear units that had been rectified. These units were far more articulate and trained much faster than logistic units. Furthermore, competitive normalization was used to eliminate secret behaviors when nearby units had stronger activities. This assisted with strength differences.

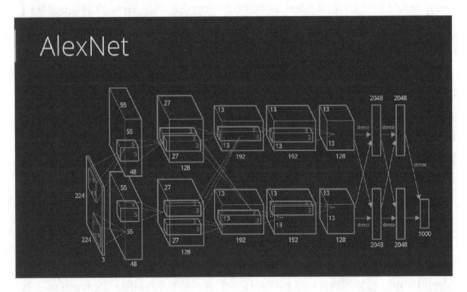

Figure 3-6. *AlexNet*

In terms of hardware, Alex used two Nvidia GTX 580 GPUs to run a very powerful implementation of convolutional nets (over 1000 fast little cores). GPUs are great for matrix-matrix multiplications and have a lot of memory bandwidth. This helps them to train the network in a week and merge findings from ten patches quickly during testing. Big neural nets can advance more than conventional CV networks as cores get cheaper and databases get larger.

Object Detection

Outputting bounding boxes and marks for specific objects is widely used to describe objects within images. This varies from the classification/ localization challenge in which classification and localization are applied to a large number of objects rather than a single dominant one. Item bounding boxes and non-object bounding boxes are the only two types of object grouping. In car detection, for example, you must detect all cars in a given picture and their bounding boxes (Figure 3-7).

Figure 3-7. *Object Detection*

We need to add a CNN to several different crops of the image if we use the sliding window technique to identify and localize images. Since CNN classifies each crop as an entity or a context, we must apply CNN to a vast range of locations and sizes, which is computationally expensive.

To deal with this, Neural Network theorists have suggested using regions instead, which are image regions that are likely to include features that are "blobby" in appearance.

This is a relatively easy game to play. R-CNN (Region-Based Convolutional Neural Network) was the first model to get it moving. In an R-CNN, we first use a selective search algorithm to scan the input image for potential artifacts, producing 2,000 area proposals (Figure 3-8). Then, on top of all these area proposals, we run a CNN. Finally, we feed each CNN's output into an SVM to identify the area and linear regression to tighten the object's bounding box.

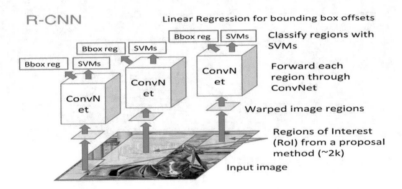

Figure 3-8. *R-CNN Network*

Essentially, we transformed the issue of object recognition into one of image classification. However, there are several drawbacks: preparation takes a long time and requires a lot of disk space, and inference is often sluggish.

Quick R-CNN is a direct descendant of R-CNN, which increases detection speed by performing two enhancements: (1) performing feature extraction before proposing areas, resulting in only running one CNN over the whole image, and 2) replacing SVM with a softmax layer, resulting in expanding the Neural Network for predictions rather than developing a new model.

Since it only trains one CNN for the whole picture, fast R-CNN performs much better in terms of speed. The selective search algorithm, on the other hand, also takes a long time to produce area proposals.

As a result, a faster R-CNN was developed, and it has since become a canonical standard for deep learning–based object detection (Figure 3-9). It inserts a Region Proposal Network (RPN) to predict proposals from features, replacing the slow selective search algorithm with a fast Neural Network. To minimize the computational requirements of the overall inference process, the RPN is used to determine "where" to look. The RPN scans each position rapidly and efficiently to decide if additional processing is needed in that region. It accomplishes this by producing K bounding box proposals, each with two scores showing the possibility of an item being present at each site.

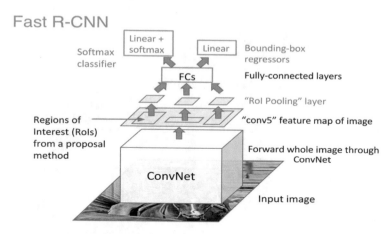

Figure 3-9. *Fast R-CNN*

We feed our area ideas directly into what is effectively a swift R-CNN once we have them. A pooling layer, several fully connected layers, a softmax classification layer, and a bounding box regressor are added at last.

Overall, faster R-CNN outperforms the competition in terms of speed and accuracy. While future models increased detection speeds dramatically, only a few models were able to outperform faster R-CNN by a substantial margin. In other words, while faster R-CNN isn't the easiest or fastest object detection process, it's still one of the most efficient (Figure 3-10).

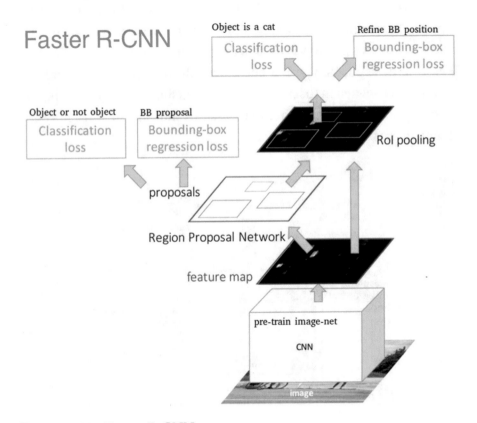

Figure 3-10. *Faster R-CNN*

In recent years, global object detection patterns have moved toward simpler and more powerful detection systems. As a step toward sharing computation on a whole picture, approaches like You Only Look Once (YOLO), Single Shot MultiBox Detector (SSD), and Region-Based Fully

Convolutional Networks (R-FCNs) were observable. As a consequence, these strategies separate themselves from the three R-CNN techniques' expensive subnetworks. The key reason behind these patterns is to stop making different algorithms concentrate on their respective subproblems in isolation, which may increase training time and decrease network precision.

The method of following a single point of interest, or several objects, in a given scene is known as object tracking (Figure 3-11). It has historically been used in video and real-world encounters where findings are made after the initial identification of an object. It is now important for autonomous driving applications such as Uber and Tesla's self-driving cars.

Figure 3-11. *Object Tracking*

According to the observation paradigm, object tracking approaches can be classified into two categories: generative and discriminative. The generative approach, such as PCA, uses a generative model to explain the visible characteristics and minimizes the reconstruction error.

The discriminative approach will differentiate between the target and the background; its accuracy is more reliable, and it is increasingly replacing the traditional tracking method. Tracking by detection is another term for the discriminative process, and deep learning falls into this group. To achieve tracking by detection, we detect candidate objects in all frames and then use deep learning to classify the target object among the candidates. Stacked autoencoders (SAEe) and Convolutional Neural Networks (CNNs) are two types of simple network models that can be used.

Deep Learning Tracker (DLT) is the most common deep network for monitoring tasks using SAE, as it allows for offline pre-training and online fine-tuning. The procedure is as follows:

- By applying noise to input images and reconstructing the original images, the stacked denoising autoencoder will achieve a more robust function expression ability.

To create the classification network, combine the coding portion of the pre-trained network with a classifier, and then fine-tune the network using the positive and negative samples collected from the original frame to discriminate the current entity from the past. DLT creates candidate patches for the current frame using a particle filter as the motion model. The classification network produces likelihood scores for these patches, which show how confident their classifications are, and then selects the highest of these patches as the object.

- DLT employs a minimal threshold approach to model updating.

CNN has become the standard deep paradigm of machine vision and visual recognition due to its dominance in image recognition and object detection. A large-scale CNN can be trained as both a classifier and a tracker, in general. A fully convolutional network tracker (FCNT) and multi-domain CNN are two examples of CNN-based tracking algorithms (MD Net).

- FCNT successfully analyzes and utilizes the function maps of the VGG model, which is a pre-trained ImageNet, yielding the following findings:

  - CNN function maps may be used for monitoring and localization.

  - For the task of distinguishing a specific object from its context, often CNN function maps are often blurred or unrelated.

  - Lower layers encode more discriminative attributes to capture intra-class variation, while higher layers capture semantic concepts on object categories.

Because of these results, FCNT builds a feature discovery network to pick the most important feature maps on the VGG network's conv4–3 and conv5–3 layers. It then creates two additional channels (called SNet and GNet) for the chosen feature maps from two layers separately to prevent overfitting on noisy ones. The GNet captures the object's category detail, while the SNet distinguishes the object from a similar-looking context.

To obtain heat maps of the object, both networks are initialized with the specified bounding box in the first frame, and for new frames, a region of interest (ROI) centered at the object position in the previous frame is cropped and propagated. Finally, the classifier receives two heat maps for prediction via SNet and GNet, and the tracker determines which heat map will be used to produce the final tracking result based on whether there are any distractors. The FCNT pipeline is illustrated in the following (Figure 3-12).

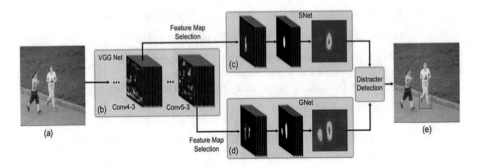

Figure 3-12. *Convolutional Network Pipeline*

Summary

This chapter covers basic math for computer vision including linear algebra and multivariable calculus. It also covers why to study computer vision. The standard algorithms covered in this chapter are image classification, object detection, instance segmentation, and object tracking. It also covers how a computer reads an image.

Image classification is the process of categorizing and labeling groups of pixels or vectors within an image based on specific rules.

Object detection is a computer vision technique that allows us to identify and locate objects in an image or video.

Semantic segmentation describes the process of associating each pixel of an image with a class label (such as flower, person, road, sky, ocean, or car).

In the upcoming chapter, we will discuss facial detection/recognition and body detection / tracking.

CHAPTER 4

Computer Vision Applications

This chapter will focus on various computer vision application, the evolution of the technology, and how to set up a C++ vision application.

Overview

In computer vision, simulating the human eye enables the computer to process and recognize things in videos and photographs in the same way as human beings, from scenery to objects, motion, and many more. Computer vision has only operated in a small capacity until recently. Today, deep learning has empowered the advanced computer vision we see in many pieces of software we use on a daily basis. In fact, one of the most popular branches of deep learning is computer vision; therefore, deep learning plays a crucial role to achieve and perform complex computer vision operations.

© Ahmed Fathi Bekhit 2022
A. F. Bekhit, *Computer Vision and Augmented Reality in iOS*,
https://doi.org/10.1007/978-1-4842-7462-0_4

If you were asked to describe the objects/things in Figure 4-1, you would likely mention that in this picture there are "juice, basket, boy, girl, man, woman, grass, etc." Then if you were asked to describe what's happening in the picture, your answer would likely be "It's a family enjoying a picnic," with very minimal effort. These are two very basic tasks that could be done by most children over the age of six or seven years. In context, it is a very complex process, however. Human vision is an extremely complex organic component of our eyesight. Our conceptual model, our concept of abstracted interpretation, and our confidential occurrence are also taken into account across billions and trillions of encounters in our lives with the universe.

Figure 4-1. *Colorful Image (RGB Image)*

The resolution of images that is rendered by digital cameras have details that far exceed the system of human vision. With very high precision, the variations in colors can also be observed and quantified. But making sense out of the content of those pictures is a challenge computers have faced for decades.

We, as humans, experience with apparent ease the three-dimensional nature of the world around us. In parallel, computer vision researchers have developed mathematical methods to restore the three-dimensional structure and appearance of objects in photography.

Applications of Computer Vision

Computer vision has its relevance in the issues it tackles. This is one of the most important developments in the digital world. Computer vision helps vehicles drive themselves and perceive their surroundings. The camera records the different angles of a car and feeds the information into the computer vision software, which then finds the road limits and traffic lights and detects the distance from other cars, pedestrians, and objects in real time by processing the images. On highways and streets, the self-driving vehicle will then navigate its way, avoid hitting barriers, and bring the travelers to their destination safely.

A common feature in computer vision is face recognition. We match the face photos of people with their identities through computer vision technology. In images, the algorithms of computer vision detect the face features and compare these to the face profiles in the database. In order to authenticate their owners' identities, consumer devices use facial recognition. In order to tag users, social media applications use facial recognition.

In computer vision, the technology that helps computer systems like tablets, smart glasses, and smartphones to overlay virtual objects in real-world pictures plays a significant role in enhanced and mixed reality. AR equipment uses computer vision to identify objects in the real world to locate a virtual object on the monitor of a device. For example, AR systems may use computer vision algorithms to detect the planes that are very important for detecting depth and measurements and for positioning.

Photo galleries online such as Google Photos use the eyes of a computer to detect and automatically categorize the photographs by subject type. You will save a lot of time than applying tags for your photographs and explanations. The technology also allows users to scan for video hours by typing into the form of content they want rather than manually watching full-length videos. Computer vision has also played a crucial role in the advancement of health science. Computer vision algorithms can aid in the medical automation tasks including identifying cancerous lumps in skin images.

Other more complex applications occur in Computer Vision. For example, imagine a smart home surveillance camera that constantly sends your home video to the cloud and allows you to display the image on a remote level. You may set up a cloud framework with computer vision in order to alert you immediately when anything suspicious occurs, anything in the house that takes fire. This will save you a great deal of time by making sure you can see your house with a watchful eye. The US military is now processing video contents recorded by cameras and drones with computer vision.

If you take a step further in this example, you would notice that the protection program only stores the videos that the vision algorithm flags abnormally. This would allow us to minimize the size of the content stored in the cloud, since the majority of your safety camera photos are innocuous in almost every case and do not need to be checked.

Before there were a few deep learning activities that computer vision could achieve, developers and human operators needed a great deal of initiative and manual coding. For example, if you wanted to recognize a face, you must taking the following steps:

1. Collect the images of each subject in a certain format by building a database. Annotate images and enter a number of data items for each picture, such as the distance from the eyes, nose bridge width, upper lip distance from the nose, and hundreds of further measures that define each person's specific characteristics.

2. Capture the images. If you are using pictures or video content, you will have to capture new files. And then the measuring process has to be revisited to mark the key points in the picture. You must also take the angle of the image.

The program will eventually match to those in the database and compare the measurements found in the new image if they fit any of the tracking profiles. In fact, the work was conducted manually, and very little automation was used, and the margin of error remained high.

Machine learning was another approach to find solutions to problems with computer vision. Developers no longer need to write code for each regulation manually in the vision applications with machine learning. The programming of the "features" instead included smaller applications that could detect such image patterns. The algorithm used then to detect trends, recognize unique features and detect objects using a statistical learning algorithm such as linear regression, decision trees and logistic regression.

Deep learning offered a totally new way of learning machines. Deep learning relies on Neural Networks, which can overcome any problem that can be illustrated by examples. A Neural Network contains many representations of a particular category of data, common patterns can be taken from these examples and converted into a mathematical equation that helps to identify potential data items.

Constructing a deep learning program only involves the selection of a pre-constructed algorithm or the creation of one with examples of the faces of the individuals it is expected to detect. The Neural Network can identify faces with appropriate examples without additional function and measuring instructions.

Deep learning is a highly powerful approach for computer vision. In certain cases, the development of a successful deep learning algorithm consists in the selection of big number of the named training data and limits such as the Neural Network form, the number of the neural layers of the network, and the number of times to train the network. Deep learning and machine learning are both easier and quicker to implement than previous forms.

Deep learning is used in most current machine vision systems such as self-driving vehicles, facial recognition, and cancer identification, with the availability and advancement of hardware and cloud computing infrastructure.

Read, Write, and Display Images

Using numbers like photographs and text, computers see and process everything. The reading and writing of pictures is important for any project of computer vision. And this work is a lot simpler with the OpenCV library.

An integer in the matrix determines the pixel intensity at that particular location. In the figure above, we are displaying the grayscale picture and its pixel value intensity equivalent on the right (Figure 4-2), in that example there is only one attribute, that is the black color intensity at a given pixel location. The function of imread in OpenCV reads the images in BRG. When implementing the imread function, we have the option to read the given image in different forms: color, grayscale, or unchanged. The list below demonstrates the actual values that needs to be passed to the function:

1. Cv2.IMREAD_COLOR

2. Cv2.IMREAD_GRAYSCALE

3. Cv2.IMREAD_UNCHANGED

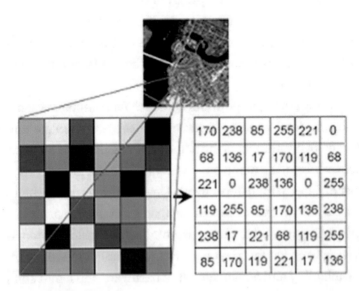

Figure 4-2. *Division of Rows and Columns in a 2D Continuous Image*

Change the Color Space

In a way that makes them conveniently reproducible, a protocol for expressing colors is a color space. A grayscale image has one pixel value for a single pixel, however color images have three values for a single pixel, that is, red (R), green (G), and blue (B) usually referred to as RGB.

In most cases, computer vision uses the RGB format to process images. Today, the OpenCV library the default format when reading and image is RGB, however it stores the image data in BGR, which is similar to RGB but it only differs in the order of the pixel description. Therefore when reading pictures with OpenCV, you must convert the image color field from BGR to RGB (Figure 4-3).

Figure 4-3. *RGB Components of an Image*

Resize the Images

A training model has a fixed input size for machine learning tasks. The same also applies to computer vision models. We should have images of the same size when training our model. OpenCV offers convenience methods allowing scaling up and down images. These methods are helpful when we need to translate images to the input form of the deep learning algorithm for its training (Figure 4-4).

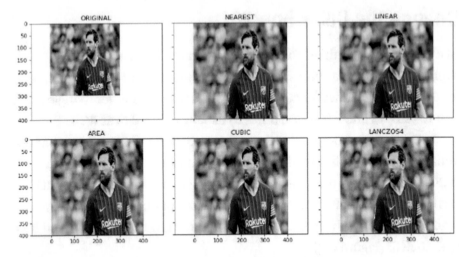

Figure 4-4. *Different Resolutions/Scales for an Image*

Rotate the Image

Data augmentation methods are among the most commonly used, and one easy-to-introduce technique in image/data augmentation is rotation (Figure 4-5). Using this technique, we will be able to build more examples for our deep learning training model. Data augmentation uses the samples of data available and builds new copies of them using rotation and translation.

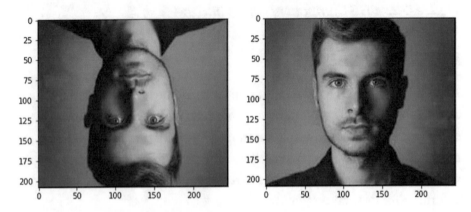

Figure 4-5. *Image Rotation*

Bitwise Operation

AND, OR, XOR, and NOT are bitwise operations. These operations are very helpful and used together with masking when we want to remove an area we wish from an input image (Figure 4-6).

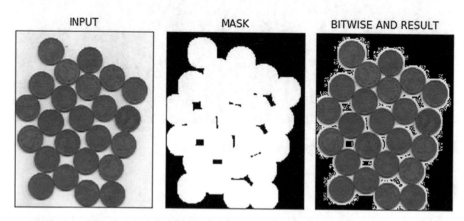

Figure 4-6. *Bitwise Operations*

We can measure the segmented mask in the image with the use of the watershed algorithm and see the image provided by us after we use the bitwise "AND" operation to eliminate the backdrop of the image and take the region we need.

Detect the Edges

Edges are very useful image features, which can be used for various purposes, such as image recognition and positioning of objects. The edge characteristics of the objects in the picture can be determined also by deep research models. They are also used to sharpen an image (Figure 4-7).

Figure 4-7. *Sharpening of an Image*

Image Filtering

To blur images, we use the Gaussian filter, which gives the neighboring pixels different weights depending on their distance from the pixel being considered (Figure 4-8).

Figure 4-8. *Original Image and Image After Gaussian Kernel*

To apply a Gaussian filter, kernels are used for image filtering. The dot product in a given portion of an image is determined using a kernel. The center of a kernel within the pixel are overlapped when the new pixel value is calculated. The nearby pixel values are multiplied by the necessary kernel values. A value that coincides with the center of the kernel is allocated with the pixel.

Detect Face

OpenCV supports object identification based on the Haar cascade. Haar cascades are classifiers based on a machine learning framework, which measure various features such as edges, lines, etc. The machine detects the face through the retina (Figure 4-9).

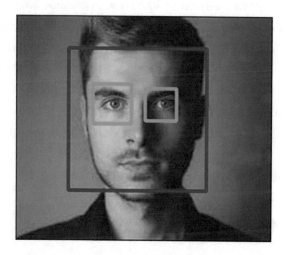

Figure 4-9. *Bounding Box for Face Detection*

Computer Vision Algorithms

The technique used to classify or identify photographs is typically represented in a set of data points that is used to predict a specific category. Image labeling is a classification sub-problem in which a whole picture is labeled a category. Using the image labeling technique, a human manually labels the whole image with a set of categories. Once we have a set of data with labeled images, we can apply a matching algorithm to compare a new non-labeled user inputted image with the dataset we have. Once a matching or similar labeled image is found, we return the appropriate set of categories.

There are countless groups in which you can classify a particular picture. Consider a manual procedure in which images are matched and identical images are sorted by like characteristics, but without understanding what you are looking for in advance. This is an onerous assignment, clearly. To make it more clear, presume that there are hundreds of thousands of images. In order to do this effectively, it is immediately obvious that an automated system is needed.

A number of tasks for classifying images require photography of objects. CIFAR-10 and CIFAR-100 are two common datasets, with pictures to be classified, respectively, into 10 and 100 groups. These datasets are industry standard and are available for the public domain.

Image Classification in Deep Learning

The architecture for deep photography recognition usually contains convolutional layers, becoming a Neural Network that is convolutional (CNN). For CNNs, it is common to have images on the network and details are divided into network categories. CNNs start with an input "scanner," and not all training data are parsed simultaneously. For example, you would not want a 10,000-node layer to process an image of 100×100 pixels. Instead, you create a 10×10 Input Layer that accepts the first 10×10 image pixels. You feed the next 10 × 10 pixels, moving the scanner 1 pixel to the right before the input is transferred. This technique makes the process more efficient.

Object Detection

Object detection is a machine vision process that finds and differentiates objects in a picture or video. The identification of objects specifically draws bounding boxes around the detected objects to locate where they are in a given scene (or to observe how they pass around it). Object identification is typically confused with image recognition, so it is important that we explain the distinctions between them before we continue. Image recognition, also referred to as Image Classification, assigns a name to the image. The mark "dog" is represented with a picture of a dog. The mark "dog" still applies to a picture of two dogs. On the other hand, target recognition draws a bounding box around each dog and names the box "dog." Which specifies where a given object is and what mark/title should be added, according to the model forecasts. In that way, object detection offers more than recognition/classification information about an image (Figure 4-10).

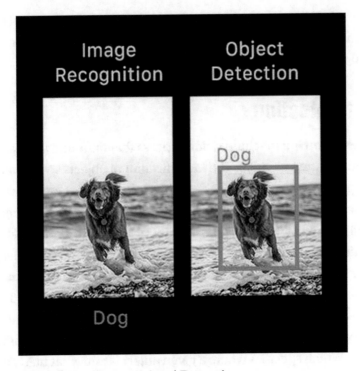

Figure 4-10. *Object Recognition/ Detection*

Object Detection Types

Goal recognition can typically be divided into machine learning approaches and deep learning approaches.

Computer vision techniques are used to identify classes of pixels, which may belong to an object, using traditional machine learning-based approaches to analyze various properties of an image, such as a color histogram or boundaries. These characteristics are then integrated into a regression model that predicts the location and name of the entity. Deep learning approaches, however, are based on Convolutional Neural Networks (CNNs) for the purposes of identification of artifacts that have to be extracted separately.

As deep learning approaches have become the modern methods of object recognition, these are the techniques that we will focus on for the purposes of this implementation.

Importance of Object Detection

Object ID is inextricably associated with other related computer vision techniques, such as pattern recognition and image segmentation, that help us to identify and perceive image or video scenes.

Nevertheless, there are underlying differences. Image detection only creates a class label for a detected object, and image segmentation provides a pixel-level description of the components of a scene. Object recognition is separated from these other practices by possessing the unique ability to recognize objects within an image or video. This then allows you to count those objects and map them with the unique ability to recognize certain primary distinctions; we can see how it can be incorporated in a variety of ways:

- Counting audience
- Cars self-driving
- Surveillance recording
- Detection of the mask

Detection of Anomaly

This is obviously not a complete list, but it includes some of the main issues through which object recognition impacts our future.

Object Tracking

In any given scene, this applies to tracking one or more moving objects (Figure 4-11). This has historically been implemented after the original object has been observed to track real-world encounters. It is a very significant part of self-driving vehicles that will be launched by companies such as Uber and Tesla. It is possible to break object detection into two categories: *generative* and *biased*. The generative approach would describe visible features and minimize reconstruction errors in the hunt for the subject.

Figure 4-11. *Object Detection Bounding Boxes*

The discriminatory process is more efficient and accurate. It can be used to tell the difference between the issue and the meaning and has been the preferred way of monitoring. It goes with the name tracking by detection.

Semantic Segmentation

The method of agglomerating portions of an image that fall under the same object class is called semantic separation or image segmentation. Each pixel of the image has a sort of pixel preview since it is categorized by category. Cityscapes, PASCAL VOC, and ADE20K are among the standards for this mission. Mean IoU and pixel precision metrics are commonly used in testing models. The mean IoU is used to test models. More precisely, the purpose of semantic image segmentation is to mark what is depicted in each pixel of an image a corresponding class. This method is widely referred to as dense prediction, since we forecast for each pixel in the image.

One important point to remember is that instances of the same class are not separated; we think just for the type of each pixel. In other words, if you have two objects in the same group in your input image, they are not automatically distinguished as separate objects by the segmentation map. A different type of model exists, known as example segmentation model, which discriminates between distinct objects of the same class.

For a number of activities, segmentation models are helpful.

Vehicles That Are Automatic

In order for self-driving cars to fit safely into our current highways, we need to equip cars with the requisite perception to consider their surroundings.

Medical Diagnostic Picture

Machines will improve the research carried out by radiologists, significantly decreasing the time needed for diagnostic testing to be carried out (Figure 4-12).

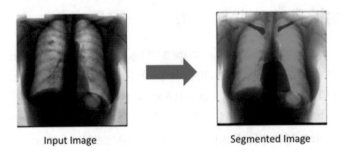

Input Image   Segmented Image

Figure 4-12. *Sample Segmented Image*

Instance Segmentation

For each recognized object within an image, instance segmentation distinguishes each instance of an object.

Segmentation of instances assigns a mark to each image pixel. It is used to count the number of items in a given image for tasks like image segmentation.

Requirements

The objective here of object detection is to identify specific objects and to place a bounding box for each entity example.

Each example is segmented. The goal is to define every pixel in a fixed set of categories without distinguishing object instances.

Mask R-CNN is a deep learning technique that expands on R-CNN by focusing more on instance segmentation.

What's new about R-CNN and faster R-CNN?

Mask R-CNN has another branch for predicting the segmentation of pixels to pixels in every field or region of interest (ROI).

R-CNN does not synchronize the input network pixels for higher speed. R-CNN produces two outputs faster:

- Class symbol

- Each applicant's offset bounding box

Three outputs of mask R-CNN are

- Class symbol

- Each applicant's offset bounding box

- Mask object

Mask R-CNN and faster R-CNN branches, for grouping and regression of boundaries are found here.

To delete the image feature, we may use the ResNet 101 deep learning architecture.

Both use the network zone proposal to establish a field of interest (RPN).

Work on Image Reconstruction

Imagine that you have an old snapshot and, over time, pieces have begun to erode. This is a very valuable photo, so you'd like to recover it. That's the restoration of pictures. In order to come up with corrupted copies of images that the models have to learn to restore and enhance, the datasets would normally contain existing pictures. With businesses such as IBM and Pinterest leading the way, both sectors are investing heavily in computer vision research. It is still important to remember that given all the strength of computer vision, since it is infamous for its black-box decision making, there are still remaining security issues. This is where people are suspicious of computers that use information to forecast their every move and make decisions on matters such as their credit risk, health status, and many other human choices. Nevertheless, with the fast growth of AI and security requirements, we should hope to address certain issues to remedy our privacy concerns.

Implementing Vision Applications

A) Face Detection/Recognition

The program here makes use of the OpenCV library for detecting a face in a web cam feed or even a video clip saved locally. The code here recognizes or monitors faces in live time. It accomplishes this with the aid of pre-trained XML classifiers. Facial features have been programmed into the classifiers used in this program. To detect various objects, classification techniques could be utilized.

To run a program, you'll need to do the following:

1. On the local computer, OpenCV must be configured.

2. Before the program can be run, the paths to the classifier XML files must be defined. The OpenCV location "OpenCV/data/haarcascades" contains these XML files.

3. When capturing, utilize "0" as the value. To run the web cam stream, type open (0).

4. Provide the path to the video file to use in face detection, *(capture.open("path to video"))*, for example.

Implementation

```
// CPP program to detects face in a video

// Include required header files from OpenCV directory
#include "/usr/local/include/opencv2/objdetect.hpp"
#include "/usr/local/include/opencv2/highgui.hpp"
#include "/usr/local/include/opencv2/imgproc.hpp"
#include <iostream>

using namespace std;
using namespace cv;

// Function for Face Detection
void detectAndDraw( Mat& img, CascadeClassifier& cascade,
                    CascadeClassifier& nestedCascade, double scale );
string cascadeName, nestedCascadeName;

int main( int argc, const char** argv )
{
    // VideoCapture class for playing video for which faces to be detected
    VideoCapture capture;
    Mat frame, image;

    // PreDefined trained XML classifiers with facial features
    CascadeClassifier cascade, nestedCascade;
    double scale=1;

    // Load classifiers from "opencv/data/haarcascades" directory
    nestedCascade.load( "../../haarcascade_eye_tree_eyeglasses.xml" ) ;
```

In this part of the code, you need to include required header files from the OpenCV directory and load classifiers.

```
// Change path before execution
cascade.load( "../../haarcascade_frontalcatface.xml" ) ;
```

After that, change the path in "cascade.load" before executing it.

```
// Change path before execution
cascade.load( "../../haarcascade_frontalcatface.xml" ) ;

// Start Video..1) 0 for WebCam 2) "Path to Video" for a Local Video
capture.open(0);
if( capture.isOpened() )
{
    // Capture frames from video and detect faces
    cout << "Face Detection Started...." << endl;
    while(1)
    {
        capture >> frame;
        if( frame.empty() )
            break;
        Mat frame1 = frame.clone();
        detectAndDraw( frame1, cascade, nestedCascade, scale );
        char c = (char)waitKey(10);

        // Press q to exit from window
        if( c == 27 || c == 'q' || c == 'Q' )
            break;
    }
}
else
    cout<<"Could not Open Camera";
return 0;
}
```

Use 0 to initiate the web cam stream. After that, face detection will start.

```
void detectAndDraw( Mat& img, CascadeClassifier& cascade,
                    CascadeClassifier& nestedCascade,
                    double scale)
{
    vector<Rect> faces, faces2;
    Mat gray, smallImg;

    cvtColor( img, gray, COLOR_BGR2GRAY ); // Convert to Gray Scale
    double fx = 1 / scale;

    // Resize the Grayscale Image
    resize( gray, smallImg, Size(), fx, fx, INTER_LINEAR );
    equalizeHist( smallImg, smallImg );

    // Detect faces of different sizes using cascade classifier
    cascade.detectMultiScale( smallImg, faces, 1.1,
                              2, 0|CASCADE_SCALE_IMAGE, Size(30, 30) );
```

This part of the code detects different sizes of faces using a cascade classifier.

```
for ( size_t i = 0; i < faces.size(); i++ )
{
    Rect r = faces[i];
    Mat smallImgROI;
    vector<Rect> nestedObjects;
    Point center;
    Scalar color = Scalar(255, 0, 0); // Color for Drawing tool
    int radius;

    double aspect_ratio = (double)r.width/r.height;
    if( 0.75 < aspect_ratio && aspect_ratio < 1.3 )
    {
        center.x = cvRound((r.x + r.width*0.5)*scale);
        center.y = cvRound((r.y + r.height*0.5)*scale);
        radius = cvRound((r.width + r.height)*0.25*scale);
        circle( img, center, radius, color, 3, 8, 0 );
    }
    else
        rectangle( img, cvPoint(cvRound(r.x*scale), cvRound(r.y*scale)),
                cvPoint(cvRound((r.x + r.width-1)*scale),
                cvRound((r.y + r.height-1)*scale)), color, 3, 8, 0);
    if( nestedCascade.empty() )
        continue;
    smallImgROI = smallImg( r );
```

This chunk of code draws a circle around the face by detecting the shape and uses a scalar color as a drawing tool.

```
nestedCascade.detectMultiScale( smallImgROI, nestedObjects, 1.1, 2,
                            0|CASCADE_SCALE_IMAGE, Size(30, 30) );
```

This detects the eyes from the input image.

```
// draw circles around eyes
for ( size_t j = 0; j < nestedObjects.size(); j++ )
{
    Rect nr = nestedObjects[j];
    center.x = cvRound((r.x + nr.x + nr.width*0.5)*scale);
    center.y = cvRound((r.y + nr.y + nr.height*0.5)*scale);
    radius = cvRound((nr.width + nr.height)*0.25*scale);
    circle( img, center, radius, color, 3, 8, 0 );
}
```

The loop here will draw a circle around the eyes.

```
        }
    }

    // Show Processed Image with detected faces
    imshow( "Face Detection", img );
}
```

The function *imshow* will process the image if the face is detected as shown in the following output image:

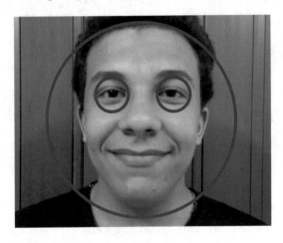

B) Body Detection/Tracking

Tracking is the process of finding an object in a video frame by frame. Although the meaning seems direct, tracking is indeed an extremely broad concept within computer vision and machine learning, which includes conceptually related yet technically distinct concepts. For instance, object tracking encompasses many of the following distinct but interrelated concepts:

Thick optic flow: Such algorithms assist in calculating the motion vector within each pixel in a video frame.

Sparse optical flow: The Kanade-Lucas-Tomasi (KLT) feature tracking is one of these algorithms that track the position from some feature points in a picture.

Kalman filtering: A common signal processing algorithm is utilized prior motion knowledge to predict the position of an object moving. The guidance of missiles was one of the first implementations of this algorithm! "The on-board computer which led the descent of the Apollo 11 lunar module to the moon had a Kalman filter," according to the article.

Meanshift and Camshift: The maxima of a density function can be found using these algorithms. They're also employed in the tracking process.

Single-object tracker: The first frame is labeled with a rectangle to show the position of the object we would like to track within this class of trackers. The tracking algorithm is then used to track the object in subsequent frames. Such trackers are typically utilized in combination with an object detector in real-world applications.

Finding multiple object tracking algorithms: When using a quick object detector, it's a good idea to detect several objects from every frame and use a tracking algorithm to figure out whether the rectangle within each frame correlates to a rectangle in the next.

Detection vs. tracking: If you've used OpenCV face detection, you find how this operates within real time or could immediately spot a face in each frame. What's the big deal about tracking within that initial position? Let us just look at why you would need to track objects in a clip rather than only doing repetitive detections.

Tracking is quicker as compared to detection: Tracking algorithms are usually quicker as compared with detection algorithms. An explanation is straightforward. While tracking an object that has been observed throughout the previous frame, we have a lot of information regarding that object's presence. We now understand the former frame's location, as well as the moving location and velocity. Thus, within the coming frame, we will utilize all this knowledge for an estimate of where an object will be within the coming frame or also conduct a tiny search across the predicted location to precisely place an object. An effective tracking algorithm can use all of the knowledge it knows regarding an object through the level, whereas a detection algorithm would always begin with a scratch. As a result, when constructing such an effective approach, the object detection algorithm being typical runs every nth frame, with the tracking algorithm used in the n-1 frames (n minus 1, where n is the total number of frames in the video). You can just track the object after detecting this within the first frame. Although tracking has advantages when we have additional data (i.e. a large set of images or a video), but it could still be dropped and missed if an object goes underneath a barrier over some longer length of time or moves too quickly for the tracking algorithm to keep it going. It's also normal for tracking algorithms to acquire bugs, as a bounding box that's tracking an object gradually moves away through this. A detection algorithm has been applied so often to solve these problems with tracking algorithms. A huge example of its object is used to train detection algorithms. As a result, they are very knowledgeable regarding an object's specific class. Tracking algorithms, across the opposite side, are most knowledgeable regarding a particular example of a class we have been tracking.

When detecting stalls, tracking will assist: When a facial detector is used in a clip but an object obscures a person's face, it would quite probably fail. A strong tracking algorithm, across either side, could deal with deformation to a certain extent.

Identification is preserved by tracking: Object detection produces a series of rectangles containing an object as an output. The item, on the other hand, has no identification. A detector that detects red dots, for example, can emit rectangles referring to every dot that has been detected in a frame as in the clip here. This would produce a new series of rectangles in the first frame. The specific dot could be portrayed with a rectangle positioned at index 10 throughout the array within a first frame, as well as at index 17 in the second frame. We have no indication which rectangle refers to which item when utilizing detection onto a single frame.

OpenCV Tracking API

OpenCV 4 includes a tracking API with configurations of such a variety for individual object tracking algorithms. BOOSTING, MIL, KCF, TLD, MEDIANFLOW, GOTURN, MOSSE, and CSRT are eight trackers included within OpenCV 4.2. In this section we will elaborate further on the differences and the pros/cons of each configuration.

To be considered: Only the following six trackers are implemented in OpenCV 3.2: BOOSTING, MIL, TLD, MEDIANFLOW, MOSSE, and GOTURN. And the following five trackers are implemented in OpenCV 3.1: BOOSTING, MIL, KCF, TLD, and MEDIANFLOW. BOOSTING, MIL, TLD, and MEDIANFLOW are the only four trackers implemented in OpenCV 3.0.

Update: The tracking API in OpenCV 3.3 has improved. When implementing the trackers, an OpenCV version check is recommended before calling the appropriate API configurations. Let's have a look at the setup and usage as we implement the tracking algorithm. To begin implementing the tracker, we start by representing the tracker options in an array to allow us to simply switch between the tracker forms – BOOSTING, MIL, KCF, TLD, MEDIANFLOW, GOTURN, MOSSE, or CSRT – as shown in the following code with comments:

```
1   #include <opencv2/opencv.hpp>
2   #include <opencv2/tracking.hpp>
3   #include <opencv2/core/ocl.hpp>
4
5   using namespace cv;
6   using namespace std;
7
8   // Convert to string
9   #define SSTR( x ) static_cast< std::ostringstream & >( \
10  ( std::ostringstream() << std::dec << x ) ).str()
11
12  int main(int argc, char **argv)
13  {
14      // List of tracker types in OpenCV 3.4.1
15      string trackerTypes[8] = {"BOOSTING", "MIL", "KCF", "TLD","MEDIANFLOW",
        "GOTURN", "MOSSE", "CSRT"};
16      // vector <string> trackerTypes(types, std::end(types));
```

At the start of the code, OpenCV and tracking libraries have to be included, and add a list of the tracker types in OpenCV 3.4.1.

```
18      // Create a tracker
19      string trackerType = trackerTypes[2];
20
21      Ptr<Tracker> tracker;
22
23      #if (CV_MINOR_VERSION < 3)
24      {
25          tracker = Tracker::create(trackerType);
26      }
27      #else
28      {
29          if (trackerType == "BOOSTING")
30              tracker = TrackerBoosting::create();
31          if (trackerType == "MIL")
32              tracker = TrackerMIL::create();
33          if (trackerType == "KCF")
34              tracker = TrackerKCF::create();
35          if (trackerType == "TLD")
36              tracker = TrackerTLD::create();
37          if (trackerType == "MEDIANFLOW")
38              tracker = TrackerMedianFlow::create();
39          if (trackerType == "GOTURN")
40              tracker = TrackerGOTURN::create();
41          if (trackerType == "MOSSE")
42              tracker = TrackerMOSSE::create();
43          if (trackerType == "CSRT")
44              tracker = TrackerCSRT::create();
45      }
46      #endif
```

In this part, a tracker has been created, and all tracker types added previously will be used.

```
47      // Read video
48      VideoCapture video("videos/chaplin.mp4");
49
50      // Exit if video is not opened
51      if(!video.isOpened())
52      {
53          cout << "Could not read video file" << endl;
54          return 1;
55      }
56
```

Here in this part of the code, the video is read, and you have to specify the path of the video file in VideoCapture.

```
57    // Read first frame
58    Mat frame;
59    bool ok = video.read(frame);
60
61    // Define initial bounding box
62    Rect2d bbox(287, 23, 86, 320);
63
64    // Uncomment the line below to select a different bounding box
65    // bbox = selectROI(frame, false);
66    // Display bounding box.
67    rectangle(frame, bbox, Scalar( 255, 0, 0 ), 2, 1 );
68
69    imshow("Tracking", frame);
70    tracker->init(frame, bbox);
71
72    while(video.read(frame))
73    {
74        // Start timer
75        double timer = (double)getTickCount();
76
77        // Update the tracking result
78        bool ok = tracker->update(frame, bbox);
79
80        // Calculate Frames per second (FPS)
81        float fps = getTickFrequency() / ((double)getTickCount() - timer);
82
83        if (ok)
84        {
85            // Tracking success : Draw the tracked object
86            rectangle(frame, bbox, Scalar( 255, 0, 0 ), 2, 1 );
87        }
88        else
89        {
90            // Tracking failure detected.
91            putText(frame, "Tracking failure detected", Point(100,80),
       FONT_HERSHEY_SIMPLEX, 0.75, Scalar(0,0,255),2);
92        }
93
94        // Display tracker type on frame
95        putText(frame, trackerType + " Tracker", Point(100,20),
       FONT_HERSHEY_SIMPLEX. 0.75. Scalar(50.170.50).2):
```

The video frames will be read here in the while loop. Then a bounding box will be created and then according to the tracker type it will be displayed on the video frame with the appropriate results.

```
97          // Display FPS on frame
98              putText(frame, "FPS : " + SSTR(int(fps)), Point(100,50),
        FONT_HERSHEY_SIMPLEX, 0.75, Scalar(50,170,50), 2);
99
100         // Display frame.
101         imshow("Tracking", frame);
102
103         // Exit if ESC pressed.
104         int k = waitKey(1);
105         if(k == 27)
106         {
107             break;
108         }
109
110     }
111 }
```

Finally, the frame is displayed on the screen after the tracking is complete and the bounding box is created. The *imshow* function handles displaying the fully rendered frame in the user interface. And the if statement handles when the exit key is pressed to cancel the tracking.

We'll look at a few various tracking algorithms throughout this portion. The aim is to gain real knowledge of each tracker, rather than a piece of deep theoretical knowledge.

To begin, I'll go through some basic tracking concepts. Our aim of tracking will be to locate an object throughout a current frame after accurately tracking it in (or approximately all) prior frames. A motion model seems to be simply a nice way of saying that you know the object's position and velocity (velocity + direction of movement) in subsequent frames. We can estimate a new position depending on the present motion model unless we are unable to detect or analyze the object; therefore it is essential to be relatively familiar what the object is to detect where it is in realtime. You may create an appearance model that describes how the object appears. To more accurately predict the position of the object, this appearance model could be utilized to search within a tiny neighborhood of the motion model's predicted location. Positive (object) and negative (context) instances are fed to a classifier to train it. Let us just take a look at how different tracking algorithms solve the online training issue.

BOOSTING Tracker

This tracker is based on an online version of AdaBoost, which is the internal algorithm of the Haar cascade–based face detector. This classifier must be conditioned for both positive and negative instances of the object during runtime. The classifier is run with each pixel in the vicinity of the previous position in a new frame, and the classifier's score is registered. The object's new position is the one with the highest score. As a result, we now have yet another positive example for the classifier. Since more frames are received, the classifier is modified with the new information.

Advantages: Its algorithm is over a decade old and still works, but I couldn't think of a better purpose to do it while there are other specialized trackers (MIL, KCF), which operate along with similar principles.

Disadvantages: Output in terms of tracking is mediocre. It doesn't always understand whenever tracking isn't working.

MIL Tracker

It is similar to the BOOSTING tracker. The major difference is that, rather than finding just the object's current position as a positive example, this searches a small community surrounding the current location for many possible positive examples. You don't specify positive and negative examples in MIL; instead, you specify positive and negative "packs." The positive bag's array of photographs isn't entirely made up of positive examples. Instead, just one picture from the optimistic bag must be a good illustration! A positive pocket, in our example, contains a patch based on the object's current position as well as patches from a small community around it.

Advantages: The result is excellent. It does not drift even more than the BOOSTING tracker, so this performs admirably when partially obscured. This might be the better tracker accessible unless you're using OpenCV 3.0. However, if you're using a later version, KCF is a good option.

Disadvantages: The error of tracking is not accurately recorded. After a complete occlusion, it does not heal.

Kernelized Correlation Filter (KCF)

The ideas discussed in the previous two trackers are expanded upon in the Kernelized Correction Filter tracker. This tracker incorporates MIL tracker's multiple positive samples that include wide interacting areas. This concurrent research defines some interesting geometric parameters, which this tracker uses to make tracking both quicker and much more precise.

Advantages: It outperforms BOOSTING and MIL in terms of accuracy and speed as well as reporting tracking failure. I suggest using this for most applications if you're using OpenCV 3.1 or higher.

Disadvantages: After a complete obstruction, it doesn't restore.

MedianFlow Tracker

From within, the detector calculates the differences among the object's forward and backward trajectories in a period. It can accurately detect tracking errors and pick accurate trajectories in clip sequences by reducing the forward/backward error. In my experiments, I discovered that this tracker works when the motion is small and predictable. This tracker can detect when the tracking has failed and stops accordingly, however other trackers continue running even if the tracking has failed.

Advantages: Outstanding reporting on monitoring failures. If a motion is predictable and there is no constriction, this technique works extremely well.

Disadvantages: When there is a lot of movement, it stalls.

GOTURN Tracker

It is the only tracking algorithm throughout the tracker class that uses a Convolutional Neural Network (CNN). We understand that OpenCV is "reliable to prospective modifications, illumination changes, and defects" with its documents.

To be considered: The Caffe model is used by GOTURN, which is a CNN-based tracker.

MOSSE Tracker

MOSSE stands for minimum output sum of squared error. While initialized with a single frame, an adaptive correlation is used for object tracking, resulting in balanced association filtering. Variations in illumination, length, and posture and non-rigid deformations do not affect the MOSSE tracker.

The maximum average ratio of the squared error is often used to identify deformation, allowing the tracker to stop and restart in which it leaves whenever the object shows up. It is indeed simple to use, reliable, as well as much quicker than other complicated trackers. However, it falls short of deep learning–based trackers in terms of accuracy.

CSRT Tracker

The spatial reliability map is used in the Discriminative Correlation Filter with Channel and Spatial Reliability (DCF-CSR) to change the filter aid to the portion of the specified location through a framework for tracking. It only makes use of two standard features (HoGs and Color Names). It also has a lower frame rate (25 fps) but has better object tracking reliability.

C) Image-to-Text Analysis

Using the C++ OCR Library, Convert an Image to Text

OCR (Optical Character Recognition) technology allows you to interpret and translate text from images or scanned documents into human-understandable text. Reading codes from coupons, creating text format-able, self-service shops, translating print information into digital versions, and so on are only a few of the applications for OCR. There seems to be a variety of OCR software and libraries on the market, but the accuracy of the OCR tests is crucial. In this section, I'll show you how to use C++ to build our own OCR software and transform images to text.

Using C++ to Convert an Image Page to Text

Let's start with a scenario in which the picture includes several lines of text. Maybe this is the case if you have a scanned book with a large number of text lines per page. In this case, the steps to transform an image to text are as follows.

In a string variable, store the image's direction.

Make a buffer to keep the OCR results in.

The aspose::ocr::page(const char *image path, wchar t *buffer, size t buffer size) function is used to perform OCR.

The results can be printed or saved to a file.

The following program example demonstrates how to use C++ to conduct OCR and transform an image to text:

```
1    std::string image_path = "sample.png";
2
3    // Prepare buffer for result (in symbols, len_byte = len * sizeof(wchar_t))
4    const size_t len = 4096;
5    wchar_t buffer[len] = { 0 };
6
7    // Perform OCR
8    size_t size = aspose::ocr::page(image_path.c_str(), buffer, len);
9
10   //Print result
11   std::wcout << buffer << L"\n";
```

Using C++, Perform Single-Line OCR on an Image

We transformed an image with multiple text lines in the previous example. When the picture only has a single line of text, such as a caption or a slogan, this may be the case. In such instances, the steps for performing OCR are as follows:

- To set the image's direction, use a string variable.

- To save the OCR data, create a buffer.

- The aspose::ocr::line(const char *image path, wchar t *buffer, size t buffer size) function is used to perform OCR.

- The OCR findings can be saved or printed.

The following code sample demonstrates how to use C++ to implement OCR on a picture with a short piece of text:

```
1   std::string image_path = "sample_line.jpg";
2
3   // Prepare buffer for result (in symbols, len_byte = len * sizeof(wchar_t))
4   const size_t len = 4096;
5   wchar_t buffer[len] = { 0 };
6
7   // Perform OCR
8   size_t size = aspose::ocr::line(image_path.c_str(), buffer, len);
9
10  //Print result
11  std::wcout << buffer << L"\n";
```

In C++, Convert a Specific Area of an Image into Text

You can also configure the API to restrict the OCR to a specific area of the image. Throughout this scenario, you can access the desired area by drawing a rectangle on the image. The steps for extracting text from a specific area of an image are as follows:

- In a variable, store the image's direction.

- Make a buffer to keep OCR results in.

- The aspose::ocr::page rect(const char *image path, wchar t *buffer, size t buffer size, int x, int y, int w, int h) function is used to perform OCR.

- The OCR results should be printed.

The following C++ code example demonstrates how to transform a specific area of an image to text:

```
1   std::string image_path = "sample_line.jpg";
2
3   // Prepare buffer for result (in symbols, len_byte = len * sizeof(wchar_t))
4   const size_t len = 4096;
5   wchar_t buffer[len] = { 0 };
6
7   int x = 138, y = 352, w = 2033, h = 537;
8
9   // Perform OCR or selected area
10  size_t size = aspose::ocr::page_rect(image_path.c_str(), buffer, len, x, y, w, h);
11
12  //Print result
13  std::wcout << buffer << L"\n";
```

CHAPTER 5

Custom Object Tracking

In this chapter how to track moving and stationary objects is covered in real time using downscaled picture details through measuring the period averaging background scene.

Overview

While working through a clip stream rather than single static pictures, we frequently have a specific object or items in mind to track across a visual field.

The basic issue of tracking in computer vision occurs in one of the two types; you will either be tracking previously identified objects or tracking unknown objects, across many scenarios, recognizing them depending on their movement.

There's also the issue of modeling moreover in tracking. At their finest, tracking strategies send us messy estimates of an object's actual location from frame to frame (Figure 5-1). Modeling helps us overcome this. In measuring a trajectory of an object evaluated messily, several effective mathematic methodologies have been made. Such strategies may be used to create two-dimensional or three-dimensional representations of objects as well as their positions.

© Ahmed Fathi Bekhit 2022
A. F. Bekhit, *Computer Vision and Augmented Reality in iOS*,
https://doi.org/10.1007/978-1-4842-7462-0_5

Figure 5-1. *Object Tracking*

Real-Time Object Tracking

The topic illustrates how to use a conventional web cam to track moving or fixed objects in real time. As objects begin to display, a simple method of tracking would be to compare the pre-specified background picture to an identical background frame. Such a situation operates within fixed environments in which you can understand a background picture despite having to track any foreground objects, for example, indoors, landings, workplaces, markets, workshops, and so on. If a paper moves or stays fixed in such a scenario across a longer length of time, one should treat it as if it is already a portion of a scenario as well as superimpose the picture toward the background to prevent additional detections. If a background object is eliminated by a scenario, the same applies. A lack of lighting and the need to adjust the cam location are both disadvantages of this method. You'll have to measure the latest background again in this scenario. A further option is to utilize edge operators for reducing adjustments in illumination. If you want to describe the object's body rather than only the outlines, you'll have to write some extra code.

Background

The conventional web cam resolution of 640 × 480 pixels is obsolete. If you plan to track very small items, you can scale this down around thrice to eliminate the distortion and greatly increase the processor speed without losing critical tracking ability. The downscaling step allows achieving great processing speeds in object tracking. When there are no objects, this runs at around a hundred frames per second on a 2 GHz single core and between 30 and 90 frames per second while there are objects. The larger the object, the longer it takes to measure every one of the blob's pixels. Except for an ImageBlobs class, the chapter, as well as code, is all dependent on former submissions.

Utilizing Code

Begin video capturing by setting up the camera as well as frames capture level while defined in Video Preview as well as Frames Captured into Memory using SampleGrabber in Buffered Mode. To begin, a background measurement method selects a background radio button. When you've selected the initiate tracking radio box to begin object tracking, every one of the recorded frames should be combined up, as well as a mean background frame, which would be calculated as stored to a JPEG file named background.jpg. I recommend that you aim the camera in a direction you would assume seeing motion. In dealing through a camera distortion or some random moving objects emerging within scenery over a brief duration measure a background for so many seconds. They will be efficiently eliminated by the mean background calculation. Initiate an object into the scenario you'd like to track, either waiting until they will emerge unless they're active.

Libraries

A mean estimation for a background frame is recommended because it helps in extracting away every distortion or small motion.

```
C++

1: background[i] = 0;
   frames_number = 0;
2: while(frames_number < N)
       background[i] = current_frame[i] + background[i];
       frames_number++;
3: background[i] = background[i] / frames_number;
```

The following classes have been added to the library:

- MotionDetector
- ImageBlobs

Instead of taking the difference among sequential frames whereas throughout a face detection article, that modifications inside the MotionDetector enable us to adjust the background frame with where a contrast would be performed for any new picture frame. ImageResize objects are used to present the background frame and the latest image frame. To begin, set a video frame size and length, including downscaling factors for the MotionDetector object:

- void MotionDetector::init(unsigned int image_width, unsigned int image_height, float zoom);

Utilize zoom = 0.125f to downscale a picture thrice. If you've completed the background calculation method, call the set background () function:

```
C++

inline int MotionDetector::set_background(const unsigned char* pBGR)
{
    return m_background.resize(pBGR);
}
```

We could now utilize the detect () function for calculating the pixels that correspond with foreground objects.

```
const vec2Dc* MotionDetector::detect(const unsigned char* pBGR)
{
    if (status() < 0)
            return 0;

    m_image.resize(pBGR);

    //RGB version
    char** r1 = m_image.getr();
    char** g1 = m_image.getg();
    char** b1 = m_image.getb();
    char** r2 = m_background.getr();
    char** g2 = m_background.getg();
    char** b2 = m_background.getb();
    for (unsigned int y = 0; y < m_motion_vector->height(); y++) {
            for (unsigned int x = 0; x < m_motion_vector->width(); x++) {
                    if (abs(r1[y][x] - r2[y][x]) > m_TH ||
                        abs(g1[y][x] - g2[y][x]) > m_TH ||
                        abs(b1[y][x] - b2[y][x]) > m_TH)
                            (*m_motion_vector)(y, x) = 1;
                    else
                            (*m_motion_vector)(y, x) = 0;
            }
    }

    //gray scale version
    /*m_difference_vector->sub(*m_image.gety(), *m_background.gety());
    for (unsigned int y = 0; y < m_motion_vector->height(); y++) {
            for (unsigned int x = 0; x < m_motion_vector->width(); x++) {
                    if (fabs((*m_difference_vector)(y, x)) > m_TH)
                            (*m_motion_vector)(y, x) = 1;
                    else
                            (*m_motion_vector)(y, x) = 0;
            }
    }*/

    m_tmp_motion_vector->dilate(*m_motion_vector, 3, 3);
    m_motion_vector->erode(*m_tmp_motion_vector, 5, 5);
    m_tmp_motion_vector->dilate(*m_motion_vector, 3, 3);

    return m_tmp_motion_vector;
}
```

You have the option of comparing RGB values or gray picture information. While converting object into gray values we considered that to be unreliable for similar shades. Erosion and dilation operations may be used to cover some holes inside the object's blobs, which may occur because of the same pixel shades inside the background and object, as well as to eliminate noise from very small motions or quite thin objects. From an ImageBlobs object, a returning vector has been utilized for blob removal. Using a class, you'll have to know about the following features.

- `void ImageBlobs::init(unsigned int width, unsigned int height);`
- `int ImageBlobs::find_blobs(const vec2Dc& image, unsigned int min_elements_per_blob = 0);`
- `void ImageBlobs::find_bounding_boxes();`
- `void ImageBlobs::delete_blobs();`

To start, set the object's size toward the downscaled picture dimensions.

(e.g., `init(zoom * image_width, zoom * image_height)`).

After that, you can start measuring blobs to find_blobs() based on the picture that was retrieved through a MotionDetector:: Detect() call to a function. A feature looks at non-zero picture vector components that are adjacent up or down, creating a blob. A currently finding blob numerical is then assigned to each component. A 10x10 vector, for instance, being utilized for the picture vector.

```
1 1 1 0 0 0 0 0 0 0
1 1 1 1 0 0 0 0 0 0
1 1 1 1 0 0 0 0 0 0
1 1 1 1 0 0 0 0 0 0
0 1 0 0 0 1 1 1 1 0
0 0 0 0 1 1 1 1 1 0
1 1 0 1 1 1 1 1 1 1
1 1 0 1 1 1 1 1 1 1
1 0 1 1 1 1 1 1 1 1
0 0 0 1 1 1 1 1 1 1
```

find_blobs() will estimate three blobs from that image. You may get the vector containing the found blobs with the const vec2Dc* ImageBlobs::get_image() const function.

```
                                                      Copy Code
1 1 1 0 0 0 0 0 0 0
1 1 1 1 0 0 0 0 0 0
1 1 1 1 0 0 0 0 0 0
1 1 1 1 0 0 0 0 0 0
0 1 0 0 0 2 2 2 2 0
0 0 0 0 2 2 2 2 2 0
3 3 0 2 2 2 2 2 2 2
3 3 0 2 2 2 2 2 2 2
3 0 2 2 2 2 2 2 2 2
0 0 0 2 2 2 2 2 2 2
```

You may utilize min_elements_per_blob to exclude minor blobs through detection (e.g., min_elements_per_blob = 5 will render the third blob undetected).

We can utilize the following methods to get at the features of found blobs:

- inline unsigned int ImageBlobs::get_blobs_number() const;
- inline const struct Blob* ImageBlobs::get_blob(unsigned int i) const;

The following is a Blob structure:

```
struct Blob {
    unsigned int elements_number;
    vector<struct Element> elements;
    unsigned int area;
    RECT bounding_box;        //[top,left; right,bottom)
};
```

Thus, elements number is the number of elements throughout the blob stored within components array of Element structures.

```
struct Element {
    vector<struct Element> neighbs;
    struct Coord coord;
};
```

A cord is indeed the component coordinate in the image vector, and neighbors include its immediately adjacent neighboring elements.

```
struct Coord {
    int x;
    int y;
};
```

While calling find blobs (), we can use find bounding boxes () to measure a bounding box among every blob contained in the RECT layout of a Blobs::bounding box screen. One must remove finding blobs with a Picture Blobs object using delete blobs () before calling find blobs () again ().

The find_blob() function is given here:

```
int ImageBlobs::find_blobs(const vec2Dc& image,
                    unsigned int min_elements_per_blob)
{
    if (m_image == 0)
    //not initialized
        return -1;

    m_image->copy(image);

    while (true) {
        struct Blob blob;
        blob.elements_number = 0;
        blob.area = 0;

        unsigned int y, x;
        //find first non-zero entry/////////////////////////////////////////
        for (y = 0; y < m_image->height(); y++) {
            for (x = 0; x < m_image->width(); x++) {
                if ((*m_image)(y, x) != 0) {
                    struct Element element;
                    element.coord.x = x;
                    element.coord.y = y;
                    blob.elements_number = 1;
                    blob.elements.push_back(element);
                    blob.area = 0;
                    memset(&blob.bounding_box, 0, sizeof(RECT));
                    break;
                }
            }
            if (blob.elements_number > 0)
                break;
        }

        if (blob.elements_number == 0) {
            mark_blobs_on_image();
            return get_blobs_number();
        }

        blob.elements.reserve(m_image->width() * m_image->height());
```

Here we will find the first non-zero entry:

```
//find blob/////////////////////////////////////////////////
unsigned int index = 0;
while (index < blob.elements_number) {
    unsigned int N = (unsigned int)blob.elements_number;
    for (unsigned int i = index; i < N; i++) {
        add_up_neighbour(blob, i);
        add_right_neighbour(blob, i);
        add_down_neighbour(blob, i);
        add_left_neighbour(blob, i);
    }
    index = N;
}
remove_blob_from_image(blob);

if (blob.elements_number > min_elements_per_blob) {
    blob.area = (unsigned int)blob.elements_number;
    blob.elements.reserve(blob.elements_number);
    m_blobs.push_back(blob);
}
}
```

Now we will find the blob in the given code.

An add * neighbor () processes look for the picture component that is identical to an ith Component within the present blob upwards, below, left, or right, then attach this towards a Blob components array:

```
inline unsigned int ImageBlobs::add_up_neighbour(struct Blob& blob, unsigned int i)
{
    const struct Element& element = blob.elements[i];
    if (element.coord.y - 1 < 0)
        return 0;
    else if ((*m_image)(element.coord.y - 1, element.coord.x) > 0) {
        struct Element new_element;
        new_element.coord.x = element.coord.x;
        new_element.coord.y = element.coord.y - 1;
        if (has_neighbour(element, new_element) == false) {
            int index = is_element_present(blob, new_element);
            if (index >= 0) {
                blob.elements[index].neighbs.push_back(element);
                return 0;
            }
            new_element.neighbs.push_back(element);
            blob.elements_number++;
            blob.elements.push_back(new_element);
            return 1;
        }
        else
            return 0;
    }
    else
        return 0;
}
```

Is_element_present () as well as has_neighbour () decide unless this same latest component has already been existing inside the blob:

```
inline int ImageBlobs::is_element_present(const struct Blob& blob,
          const struct Element& new_element) const
{
    //int index = 0;
    for(int i = (int)blob.elements_number - 1; i >= 0; i--) {
        const struct Element& element = blob.elements[i];
        if (element.coord.x == new_element.coord.x &&
            element.coord.y == new_element.coord.y) {
                //wprintf(L" %d\n", blob.elements_number - 1 - i);
                return i;
        }
        //if (++index > 2)  //inspect at least 2 last elements
        //          break;
    }
    return -1;
}

inline bool ImageBlobs::has_neighbour(const struct Element& element,
          const struct Element& new_element) const
{
    unsigned int N = (unsigned int)element.neighbs.size();
    if (N > 0) {
        for (unsigned int i = 0; i < N; i++) {
            if (element.neighbs[i].coord.x == new_element.coord.x &&
                element.neighbs[i].coord.y == new_element.coord.y)
                return true;
        }
        return false;
    }
    else
        return false;
}
```

Conclusions

I've chosen a fixed background (Figure 5-2) as well as conducted a few object tracking tests using items in front of me. The background that I utilized is shown in the following. This became averaged across a long amount of duration.

Figure 5-2. *Background*

At 66.67 frames per second, two items (display cleaners as well as mobile devices) were tracked (Figure 5-3).

Figure 5-3. *Object Tracking in Videos*

At 71.43 frames per second, a mobile energy connector was tracked (Figure 5-4). Since the cord seems to be so thin, it is not observed by erosion and dilation technicians.

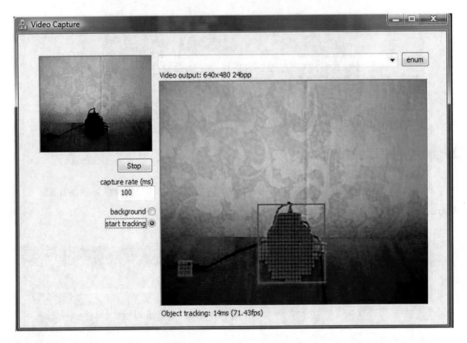

Figure 5-4. *Object Tracking in Videos*

The following is for a few pens as well as locks: 90.91 frames per second (Figure 5-5).

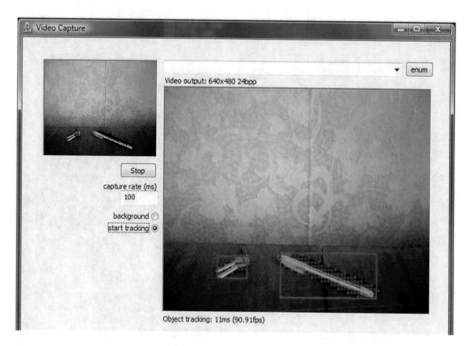

Figure 5-5. *Tracking Different Objects*

Three distinct items were observed at 29.41 frames per second in a quite complicated situation (Figure 5-6).

Figure 5-6. *Tracking Different Objects*

At 55.56 fps, a Jimi Hendrix and a 9v power were tracked (Figure 5-7).

Figure 5-7. *Tracking Different Objects*

Other background configurations are as follows (Figure 5-8):

Figure 5-8. *Another Complex Background*

At 90.91fps, numerous 9v batteries, rolling upon on rug, were observed (Figure 5-9). Due to a limitation on the quantity of components, a battery was kept unobserved.

Figure 5-9. *Another Complex Background*

At 90.91 frames per second, a battery connector, LCD-TFT filter, and 9v battery were observed (Figure 5-10). A minuscule one went unobserved once more, this time because of erosion and dilation technicians.

Figure 5-10. *Another Complex Background*

Then after 83.33 fps, candles as well as cellphones were observed (Figure 5-11).

Figure 5-11. *Another Complex Background*

As you'll observe a larger entity, much longer it takes to measure a blobs' components. It also doesn't deal with shadows by objects upon on white back wall as well as a table. Highly prominent reflections, but on the other hand, would be tracked as being related to the item.

Points of Concern

One could enhance an algorithm for tracking the location of an object's bounding box. One can insert an area toward the background scenario photo if it would be fixed for a set duration, as a result, an object being integrated into the scenario. (For example, few objects move to a scenario but remain constant.)

Custom Barcode Generator/Reader
Utilizing C++, Build and Read Barcodes

We'll show you how to programmatically create barcodes in C++ within the chapter. You'll also discover ways to build a barcode reader or scanner in the C++ program (Figure 5-12).

Figure 5-12. *Custom Barcode Reader*

Information is visually represented in the format in which machines can read it using barcodes. Innovation has proven to be beneficial in such a variety of applications, including automatic check systems within shops as well as in markets. A barcode can now be used on most commercial products. The barcode's increasing success has led to new applications across several fields. Aspose introduced a barcode generator and reader API for different channels a couple of years back, recognizing the importance of barcodes. The purpose of this chapter is to demonstrate how to automatically produce and interpret barcodes using the barcode generator and reader in C++ programs.

API for Producing and Reading Barcodes in C++

Assume, barcode with C++ is indeed a functionality C++ API that allows users to build and read a wide range of 1D as well as 2D barcodes. It allows you to produce, configure, as well as send greater-quality pictures through barcodes.

The following is a list of barcode symbologies that Aspose.BarCode with C++ will generate:

- Code128

- Code39 Standard

- Code39 Extended

- Code93 Standard

- Code93 Extended

- Code11

- Codabar

- BooklandEAN

- EAN13

- EAN8

- EAN128

- Interleaved2of5

- Standard2of5

- MSI

- Postnet

- Planet

- UPCA

- UPCE

- EAN14(SCC14)

- SSCC18

- ITF14

- BarCode supplement

- Pdf417

- QR

- Datamatrix

- Matrix 2 of 5

- PZN (Pharma Zentral Nummer, Pharmazentralnummer barcode)

- Deutsche Post Identcode

- Aztec

- Australia Post

Generating a Barcode Using C++

Utilizing Aspose to build a barcode: With only a few code lines, you can create a barcode. The measures to execute this procedure include the following:

- Make an object of a Barcode Generator class.

- Start an object with encode form and text of the barcode.

- Use the Barcode Generator->Save (System::String) process, and build a barcode.

The following code demonstration illustrates how to produce a barcode in C++:

```
const System::String codeText = u"1234567";
const System::String fileName = u"code39_barcode.jpg";
// Create barcode generator
System::SharedPtr<BarcodeGenerator> barcodeGenerator = System::MakeObject<BarcodeGenerator>(EncodeTypes::Code39Standard, codeText);
barcodeGenerator->get_Parameters()->set_Resolution(300);
// Generate barcode and save as image
barcodeGenerator->Save(fileName);
```

The barcode we produced with the previous code is shown in the following (Figure 5-13):

Figure 5-13. *Custom Barcode Reader*

Utilizing C++, Produce a 2D Barcode (QR or Other)

We generated a one-dimensional barcode in the earlier instance. Let's make a two-dimensional barcode, similar to a QR code. The steps for making a QR barcode are as follows:

- Make an object of a Barcode Generator class.

- Encode Types:: is used to configure the object. Set the text for the QR code.

- Use the Barcode Generator->Save (System::String) process, and create a barcode picture.

The following code demonstration illustrates how to create a QR barcode with C++:

```
const System::String codeText = u"1234567";
const System::String fileName = u"QR_Code.jpg";
// Create barcode generator
System::SharedPtr<BarcodeGenerator> barcodeGenerator = System::MakeObject<BarcodeGenerator>(EncodeTypes::QR, codeText);
barcodeGenerator->get_Parameters()->set_Resolution(300);
// Generate barcode and save as image
barcodeGenerator->Save(fileName);
```

By using this code, the QR code will indeed be produced.

With C++, Create and Customize Barcodes

You may also adjust the barcode's display. You may change the foreground color, background color, scale, boundary type, and other options, for instance. The methods for customizing barcodes with Aspose.BarCode with C++ are listed in the following.

- Make an object of a Barcode Generator class.

- The Barcode Generator->get Parameters () methodologies are used to reach the barcode specifications.

- Define the specifications that you like.

- Make a barcode as well as save it as a photo.

The following coding demonstration illustrates how to create a personalized barcode in C++:

```
System::SharedPtr<BarcodeGenerator> barcodeGenerator = [&] { auto tmp_0 = System::MakeObject<BarcodeGenerator>(EncodeTypes::Aztec, System::String(u"1234567890"));
// set broder style
tmp_0->get_Parameters()->get_Border()->set_DashStyle(Aspose::BarCode::BorderDashStyle::Solid);
// set width
tmp_0->get_Parameters()->get_Border()->get_Width()->set_Millimeters(1.0f);
// set border visibility
tmp_0->get_Parameters()->get_Border()->set_Visible(true);
// set background color
tmp_0->get_Parameters()->set_BackColor(System::Drawing::Color::get_Black());
// set barcode's bar color
tmp_0->get_Parameters()->get_Barcode()->set_ForeColor(System::Drawing::Color::get_Orange());
// set border color
tmp_0->get_Parameters()->get_Border()->set_Color(System::Drawing::Color::get_Black());
// set text color
tmp_0->get_Parameters()->get_Barcode()->get_CodeTextParameters()->set_Color(System::Drawing::Color::get_Orange());
// set image resolution
tmp_0->get_Parameters()->set_Resolution(400);
return tmp_0; }();

barcodeGenerator->Save(System::String(u"custom_barcode.jpg"));
```

The customizable Aztec barcode we created is shown in the following (Figure 5-14):

Figure 5-14. *Customizable Aztec Barcode*

Utilizing C++, Create Barcodes with Subtitles

The caption can appear below or above the barcode. The caption's content and appearance throughout the barcode picture can also be customized. The following code example illustrates how to build a barcode with captions in C++:

```
System::SharedPtr<BarcodeGenerator> generator = [&] { auto tmp_0 = System::MakeObject<BarcodeGenerator>(EncodeTypes::Code39Standard,
System::String(u"1234567890"));
// set caption above
tmp_0->get_Parameters()->get_CaptionAbove()->set_Text(u"Caption Above");
// set visibility
tmp_0->get_Parameters()->get_CaptionAbove()->set_Visible(true);
// set caption below
tmp_0->get_Parameters()->get_CaptionBelow()->set_Text(u"Caption Below");
// set visibility
tmp_0->get_Parameters()->get_CaptionBelow()->set_Visible(true);
// set resolution
tmp_0->get_Parameters()->set_Resolution(300);
return tmp_0; }();
generator->Save(System::String(u"barcode_caption.jpg"));
```

Figure 5-15. *A Barcode Containing Captions Up and Down Can Be Seen Here*

Utilizing C++, Scanning and Reading Barcodes

Let's look at how to use Aspose.BarCode for C++ to scan and read barcodes. The procedure using this function is as follows:

- Make an entity from the Barcode Reader class.

- Make a Barcode Reader example including the picture files for the barcode and its symbology.

- To get the text or form of the barcode, use the Barcode Reader->Read () tool.

The following programming example demonstrates how to search and interpret a barcode in C++:

```
// Create instance of BarcodeGenerator class
System::SharedPtr<BarCodeReader> reader = System::MakeObject<BarCodeReader>(u"Code128.png", DecodeType::Code128);
while (reader->Read())
{
        // Display code text and Symbology Type
        System::Console::WriteLine(System::String(u"CodeText: ") + reader->GetCodeText());
        System::Console::Write(System::String(u"Symbology Type: ") + reader->GetCodeType());
}
reader->Close();
```

C++ Is Used to Read Barcodes with Several Symbologies

In the majority of the cases, a picture just includes one barcode symbology. Even so, a picture can include barcodes from several symbologies throughout a relatively similar period in certain cases. You should have a collection of barcode symbologies to have been scanned as well as read in such situations. The following program example demonstrates how to use C++ for scanning a picture with several barcode symbologies:

```
// Set barcode symbologies
System::ArrayPtr<System::SharedPtr<BaseDecodeType>> objArray = System::MakeArray<System::SharedPtr<Aspose::BarCode::BarCodeRecognition::BaseDecodeType>>({
DecodeType::Code39Standard, DecodeType::Pdf417 });

// Initialize the BarCodeReader, Call Read() method in a loop and  Display the codetext and symbology type
System::SharedPtr<BarCodeReader> reader = System::MakeObject<BarCodeReader>(u"RecognizingMultipleSymbologies.png", objArray);
while (reader->Read())
{
        System::Console::WriteLine(System::String(u"Codetext: ") + reader->GetCodeText());
        System::Console::WriteLine(System::String(u"Symbology type: ") + reader->GetCodeType());
}
reader->Close();
```

Summary

You studied how to use C++ to build barcodes of various symbologies in this chapter. Scanning and reading of barcodes were covered, with C++ code examples. The documents will help you to understand all regarding an API.

CHAPTER 6

Augmented Reality Using OpenCV

The chapter explains how to track moving and static objects in real time using downscaled picture details through measuring the period averaging background scene.

Overview

Augmented reality, also known as AR, is a type of technology that allows us to see virtual objects and details inside our visual field. We could get details on the objects that we can visualize with augmented reality. This improves the screen by incorporating real-world components. If I point my mobile at a street, for instance, this will provide me with additional info like the names of restaurants, fitness centers, physicians, and so on. A real-time combination of digital knowledge with the person's world is known as augmented reality. Users can interact with virtual objects in their natural surroundings by using augmented reality technologies. A person who is wearing virtual reality glasses either uses a phone or tablet screen to see details regarding any objects they have been viewing.

Three different types of AR are discussed here.

© Ahmed Fathi Bekhit 2022
A. F. Bekhit, *Computer Vision and Augmented Reality in iOS*,
https://doi.org/10.1007/978-1-4842-7462-0_6

Marker-Based AR

A digital world is interconnected with the physical world. We have to know that the user is aiming the camera at the specific page to display an educational animation directly onto the paper of a journal. As a result, the system initially should detect which page you are viewing from the live view of the camera. It would be accomplished by using a unique image or form on the page. The image would be identified, and the animation will begin right away, tracking toward the correct location on the page. A user also can switch that actual book across to see if the virtual world adheres toward the page's real surface. A marker is the name given to the recognizable image that the system identifies. Almost everything could be used as a marker as long as it has sufficiently distinct visual features.

Marker-Less AR

The virtual objects are moved by the user. Consider an augmented reality technology that allows you to put virtual furniture in a sitting room. It enables us to experiment with different object designs, as well as location combos. A client must determine where to position the virtual object within such a procedure. It is referred to as "marker-less AR."

Location-Based AR

A virtual world exists in the real world.

Augmented reality technology is connected to a particular location through location-based AR. Assume walking down a public path you're unfamiliar with seeing a virtual street sign showing the street name from your smartphone camera, and that is location-based AR. And, much the same as our AR City application, this helps you to move toward the location by overlaying routes over top of the actual paths in front of you.

Marker-Based Augmented Reality

Using ArUco Markers in OpenCV (C++) to Create Augmented Reality

Throughout this section, we'll go over what ArUco markers are as well as how to utilize them with OpenCV to perform basic augmented reality activities. For a long time, ArUco markers have been utilized in virtual reality, camera posing prediction, and calibration. Let us just take a closer look at it.

What Are ArUco Markers?

ArUco stands for Augmented Reality University of Cordoba (Figure 6-1). The University of Cordoba is a university in Cordoba, Spain, where it was made.

Figure 6-1. *ArUco Marker*

Few examples follow:

The ArUco marker is a fiducial marker that is positioned onto the photographed item as well as a scenario. It's a binary square having a dark background as well as borders, as well as a white produced pattern that

113

recognizes this. The dark borders make it much easier to see. It is available in a range of sizes. For effective detection, the size is selected depending upon the size of the object as well as the scenario. While quite minor markers aren't being identified, simply growing their size will help them to be found.

A concept will be to scan such markers as well as use them in real life. Photographing the natural world allows you to identify these markers especially. When you're a beginner, you might be wondering, "How does this help me?" Let us just glance at a few examples. We placed the printed as well as the markers, mostly on edges of the image frame throughout the instance they mentioned throughout the article. So, when markers are specifically identified, you can substitute an image frame through either a picture or clip. Once you switch the camera, a new image seems to have the right viewpoint distorted. Such markers could be placed across a route of a warehouse both fitted with a camera inside a robotics application. Since each marker seems to have a unique ID, we recognize where markers are positioned inside the warehouse. Whenever the robot's camera identifies any of these markers, this can pinpoint the exact position within a warehouse.

Using OpenCV to Create ArUco Markers

Utilizing OpenCV, we can quickly produce such markers. There are 25 predefined vocabularies for markers inside the aruco module of OpenCV. The dictionary's markers all include the same block size orbits (44, 55, 66, or 77), so every vocabulary has a set number of markers (50, 100, 250, or 1000).

Here is the C++ code that shows how to identify and generate Aruco markers. We have to use the aruco module. PredefinedDictionary in the code shows how dictionaries of 250 markers will be loaded.

C++

```
1  // Import the aruco module in OpenCV
2  #include <opencv2/aruco.hpp>
3
4  Mat markerImage;
5  // Load the predefined dictionary
6  Ptr<cv::aruco::Dictionary> dictionary =
   aruco::getPredefinedDictionary(cv::aruco::DICT_6X6_250);
7
8  // Generate the marker
9  aruco::drawMarker(dictionary, 33, 200, markerImage, 1);
```

The preceding drawMarker function allows us to select a marker with a specific ID (the second parameter – 33) out of a set of 250 markers with IDs ranging from 0 to 249. The size of the marker produced is determined by the drawMarker function's third parameter. It might produce a 200 × 200-pixel picture throughout the preceding instance. The object that will be used to preserve the created marker would be the fourth parameter (preceding markerImage). Eventually, a density parameter refers to the number of blocks that should be inserted as a boundary toward the formed binary pattern. Inside the illustration earlier, a 1-bit border would be inserted across the 66% produced shape, resulting in a 77% bit picture in a 200 × 200-pixel picture (Figure 6-2). The preceding code will produce a marker similar to the one shown in the following.

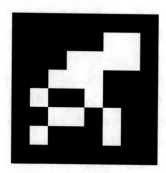

Figure 6-2. *Sample Marker*

For most cases, we'll need to create several markers, print them out, as well as position them inside the scenario.

ArUco marker detection: We must identify the ArUco markers and then utilize them in additional analysis until a scenario has been visualized by it. We'll show you how to spot the markers in the following.

C++

```
1  // Load the dictionary that was used to generate the markers.
2  Ptr<Dictionary> dictionary = getPredefinedDictionary(DICT_6X6_250);
3
4  // Initialize the detector parameters using default values
5  Ptr<DetectorParameters> parameters = DetectorParameters::create();
6
7  // Declare the vectors that would contain the detected marker corners and the
   rejected marker candidates
8  vector<vector<Point2f>> markerCorners, rejectedCandidates;
9
10 // The ids of the detected markers are stored in a vector
11 vector<int> markerIds;
12
13 // Detect the markers in the image
14 detectMarkers(frame, dictionary, markerCorners, markerIds, parameters,
   rejectedCandidates);
```

To begin, we load a similar vocabulary that has been used to create a marker. DetectorParameters is used to detect a starting collection of parameters: make something (). We can adjust numerous parameters within the identification phase using OpenCV. The default parameters function well in most situations, and OpenCV suggests that you use them. As a result, we'll keep the same settings. Four side points of a marker are identified with each active marker detection, of the sequence top left, top right, bottom right, and bottom left. Such rectangular pointers being processed as a vector of points in C++, as well as several markers throughout the picture were combined into a vector of vectors of points. A detectMarkers feature is utilized to find and detect markers' corners. The picture of the scenario with the markers will be the first parameter. The dictionary utilized to create markers is the second parameter. Markers that were accurately identified would be saved as markerCorners, or their IDs will be saved in markerIds. Also sent as a parameter seems to be the DetectorParameters entity that was created earlier. Eventually, the disqualified members are kept in the rejected candidates database.

It's critical to leave a white border across the black boundary of the markers whenever printing, cutting, and inserting them within the scene so that they could be conveniently identified.

An Augmented Reality Application

An ArUco marker has been designed for overcoming an issue for estimating camera posture for just a wide range of apps, such as augmented reality. We'll use them in this section for an augmented reality app that allows us to superimpose every current scenario upon a current picture or a clip. We choose a scenario at houses with such a huge image frame which we would like to substitute to the latest ones to view how they appear on a surface. We after which attempt to embed a clip into a film. We do this by printing, cutting, and pasting wide ArUco markers onto the picture region's edges, as seen in the picture here, and afterward recording a clip. The clip that's been taken can be found on the left side of the video at the top of the page. After that, we handle each frame of the video one by one. A marker first is detected for each picture. The identified markers are shown in green in the following image. A tiny red ring denotes the first point. By clockwise navigating a marker's boundary, you can get to the second, third, and fourth stages.

To compute a homography, four corresponding points inside the input picture as well as a current scenario picture are utilized (Figure 6-3). Under one of our previous posts, we discussed homography. Homography is indeed a transformation mapping and a referring point to another given intersection point within differing opinions of the scenario.

Figure 6-3. *Augmented Reality Using ArUco Markers in OpenCV*

A homography metric is utilized throughout the example to warp the new scenario picture through into a quadrilateral identified by the markers in the clicked picture. In the following code, we demonstrate how to do so.

C++

```cpp
1   // Compute homography from source and destination points
2   Mat h = cv::findHomography(pts_src, pts_dst);
3
4   // Warped image
5   Mat warpedImage;
6
7   // Warp source image to destination based on homography
8   warpPerspective(im_src, warpedImage, h, frame.size(), INTER_CUBIC);
9
10  // Prepare a mask representing region to copy from the warped image into the
    original frame.
11  Mat mask = Mat::zeros(frame.rows, frame.cols, CV_8UC1);
12  fillConvexPoly(mask, pts_dst, Scalar(255, 255, 255));
13
14  // Erode the mask to not copy the boundary effects from the warping
15  Mat element = getStructuringElement( MORPH_RECT, Size(3,3) );
16  erode(mask, mask, element);
17
18  // Copy the masked warped image into the original frame in the mask region.
19  Mat imOut = frame.clone();
20  warpedImage.copyTo(imOut, mask);
```

The source points (pts src) are the current scenario picture edge point, and the endpoint positions (dst src) are matching image center points inside the photo frame within the clicked picture. The homography function 'h' among an input as well as target points is computed using the OpenCV function findHomography. A current picture would then be warped to blend into the targeted frame using the homography matrix. A masked and replicated distorted picture is pasted into the intended frame. That phase has been continued within each frame in the clip.

Marker-Less Augmented Reality Using Visual-Inertial Estimation on a Phone

A live view of a real-world environment is combined with computer-generated virtual content in Augmented Reality (AR). Real-time six-degree-of-freedom (6-DoF) motion tracking is required for the registration of virtual scenes with the real world in mobile augmented/virtual reality (AR/VR). Even so, due to the limited computational ability of today's mobile terminals, the user experience in mobile AR/VR will be harmed by the delay between consecutive arriving poses. The real-time accuracy of arriving poses for mobile AR/VR is achieved using high-frequency and passive outputs from the inertial sensor. Furthermore, the robustness of conventional visual-only-based motion tracking has been improved, resulting in improved mobile AR/VR efficiency when motion blur is present. Furthermore, an adaptive filter system is developed to cope with different motion situations automatically, allowing real-time 6-DoF motion tracking by balancing the jitter and latency during the visual-inertial fusion. An AR system faces specific obstacles, such as the need for a high-quality camera pose estimate and the need to operate on platforms with minimal resources. Mobile AR aims to make a virtual object in a real-world context with an accurate pose. The device must be able to determine where the user is and what they are looking at using mobile computing.

On the other hand, mobile VR allows for a variety of interactions and connections between the user and the virtual world. Here, we present a complete system based on a hybrid approach that uses ORB binary features and optic flow to operate in near real time on a consumer tablet computer. As a result, one of the most relevant problems in mobile AR/VR is pose tracking, which involves measuring the user's position and orientation in real time. Even so, due to mobile devices' limited computing capabilities, real-time motion tracking for mobile AR/VR remains a bottleneck. The marker-based or model-based methods can only perform 6-DoF tracking with some previous knowledge of the scene, while marker-less motion tracking can operate in any situation. As a result, marker-less tracking will become more common in mobile AR/VR in the future.

Even so, the applicability and robustness of real-time 6-DoF markerless motion monitoring for mobile AR/VR still require further research due to high computing demands and volatile environments. The device employs an adaptive map of features to increase the number of ORB features that can be used. A "map" is described as a list of feature descriptors and their 3D world coordinates. So each map has a three-dimensional bounding box made up of four world coordinates. Once the camera pose has been calculated, this bounding box can be projected into the picture frame.

Sensor fusion–based 6-DoF motion tracking for mobile AR/VR in real time is realized by integrating a monocular camera and an inertial sensor. An adaptive filter architecture is proposed to balance the jitter and latency phenomenon during visual-inertial fusion, allowing real-time and smooth 6-DoF motion tracking for mobile AR/VR. Here, we show how real-time efficiency can be achieved with platform-specific optimizations proposed, as well as the use of two existing pose estimation algorithms to increase tracking speed and range. Tracking the user's posture is also essential if we want to build a sense of presence in a synthetic VR world. The device will display the virtual world from the user's perspective, thanks to the details about the user's 6-DoF pose. Simultaneous localization and mapping (SLAM), a common marker-less tracking method, can detect the 6-DoF pose of a moving camera in an unready environment, allowing phone AR/VR apps without fiducial markers.

Augmented Reality (AR) Subclass of VR

Virtual Reality (VR) has a subclass called Augmented Reality (AR). All sensory feedback received by the user is simulated in true virtual reality applications. In augmented reality, virtual content is mixed with real-world sensory feedback to produce a combined version of the environment. It is most commonly accomplished by today's consumer-grade mobile devices. The system is capable of real-time performance, analyzing live video input from a handheld camera or a head-mounted display (HMD) using computer vision techniques to assess the camera's position and orientation (pose) in 3D space. Using this pose data, virtual augmentations can be seamlessly incorporated into the real-world video stream. Marker-less AR may be used for more ubiquitous and ad hoc applications. Marker-less AR systems, rather than relying on artificial markers, make use of natural features currently existing in the environment. The most difficult aspect of marker-less AR is approaching the computational demands of camera pose estimation through natural feature detection and matching. This problem is critical in handheld mobile devices. A calibrated monocular is all that is needed for the device to work.

Almost every process, including map production, is done online and in real time, which has limited processing speeds and memory. For each point of the pipeline, the computational constraints of mobile devices are discussed, and an Android implementation is being used to test the system as a whole. When a sufficient number of good matches are found, the device attempts to estimate the camera's pose using the map's known 3D coordinates and 2D frame positions. While deciding on pose, two scenarios are considered: pose from descriptor matches and pose from tracked inliers, one for each mode of the hybrid system. It is still possible for false positives to exist despite the various limitations and thresholds implemented during the matching process. Such bad matches can make up a large portion of the correspondences, and if they aren't discarded, the recovered camera pose's accuracy suffers. The target is to calculate the pose using only correct matches. The maximum number of iterations is calculated by trial and error. Since the RANSAC algorithm is not probabilistic, the camera pose's credibility is highly dependent on the likelihood of selecting four correct points' correspondences in the maximum number of iterations possible. While there is an infinitesimal risk of failing to find inliers after 5000 iterations, the running time will be much too long.

After the map has been modified, the last step is to return the recovered pose to OpenGL, where it will be used to generate a model-view matrix. Any 3D augmentation can be drawn using a model-view matrix obtained from an accurate camera pose. With enough 3D graphics knowledge, one might create complex augmentations that blend in with their real environments. Our system's algorithms are compared to other candidate algorithms, with special attention paid to execution speed. The laptop tests are carried out to demonstrate the efficiency gap between current laptops and smartphones/tablets. The speed of image decoding is tested for three implementations – CPU-based floating-point and integer conversions, as well as our NEONaccelerated integer-based conversion – since optic flow is unaffected by the detector used.

Estimation

It is simple to locate the tracked features at first to calculate. The system's two pose estimation methods (iterative and EPnP) are compared in terms of time. Because the iterative method is only used in least-squares estimation when monitoring, this is easy. The number of RANSAC iterations performed before an appropriate pose is found determines the computation time for EPnP. As the purpose of every AR system is to create a smooth and interactive user experience, the following images display the system in action via live screen captures from the user's perspective. A 3D cube is augmented at three different sizes, as well as from an oblique angle, in the top row. Three separate maps are recognized in the bottom row, with various colors of triangles drawn depending on which map has been tracked. A marker-less virtual reality system can be used in real time on today's mobile devices.

ORB Function Detector

The ORB function detector will be implemented using NEON and the SIMD engine as the most imminent future work. If the system's previous NEON implementations are any indication, this would significantly increase the system's worst-case execution speed and may even enable feature matching to be done on top of optic flow tracking to provide a more robust pose estimate. Furthermore, as mobile hardware advances, acceleration methods used in PC implementations will become more important. Parallelization via GPU is a common way to boost algorithm performance and speed. NVidia recently unveiled the Tegra 4 processor, which will include a programmable 72–CUDA core GPU, enabling

CUDA implementations to run on cellular phones. Additional features can be added as performance improves. Currently, the device is unable to recognize multiple maps in a single camera frame; instead, it will choose the map with the highest lookup score. Following the selection of possible maps, the descriptor matching and pose estimation processes will be applied to each one separately. Because of NEON acceleration, the matching phase is rapid enough that it can be repeated several times without affecting output significantly.

Even though pose estimation is much slower, the effect of doing it several times could be mitigated by using NEON or GPU acceleration to speed up feature detection. This will result in several camera poses, each of which would have been sent back to OpenGL and augmented separately. Furthermore, real-time camera tracking performance is needed to implement SLAM technology for mobile AR/VR. Frequency of arriving poses for mobile AR should be at least as high as a standard video frame rate (25 Hz) that is usually specified as a standard regulation for real-time output. This norm is also taken into account in this document for non-mobile VR real-time outputs. Since mobile VR provides better real-time efficiency than traditional scenarios, the 6-DoF motion tracking arriving frequency should be at least 60 Hz. Only in this manner will the individual in the VR setting have a pleasant experience. Otherwise, the user will be disgusted by the delay concept in VR environments. To our understanding, there is no full AR system that incorporates all of the components discussed in this book when operating in real time on mobile devices. Online map development and multiple-map support are two features that are currently missing from existing systems.

SLAM Process

The specific SLAM process, on the other hand, involves calculating the entire image's photometric error, performing a dense (all pixels in the image) or semi-dense (high gradient areas) reconstruction while tracking the camera, and GPU acceleration is needed for real-time performance due to the computational expense. Market mobile devices' processing capabilities are inadequate for direct real-time camera monitoring. Aside from its high performance, feature-based SLAM is also thought to be more reliable than direct SLAM. As a result, the visual-based monitoring approach in this document is the feature-based SLAM system. These real-time monitoring techniques, though, were only tested on a computer. To create a mobile device that can monitor motion in real time, we incorporate various image processing techniques to detect key features in a given set of frames to find the differentiators by yielding the homography matrix.

Even so, such visual-only tracking methods suffer from poor features or motion blur, making it difficult to monitor important image features. Furthermore, the frame rate requirement for mobile VR is much greater than for smartphone AR to mitigate the dizziness phenomenon in a simulated world. As a result, the preceding visual-only tracking approaches are ineffective for both smartphone AR and VR. Other sensors can be used to further increase the robustness and frame rate of motion tracking for mobile AR/VR.

The inertial sensor can provide high-frequency and passive measurements for pose estimation as a primary motion capture sensor. The 6-DoF motion monitoring through visual-inertial fusion has been summarized by some researchers. Sensor fusion solutions can be classified as tightly coupled or loosely coupled based on various fused frameworks. Tightly coupled approaches can conduct systematic fusion of visual and Inertial Measurement Unit (IMU) measurements, which typically adds complexity, while loosely coupled approaches optimize visual and IMU monitoring separately, resulting in lower computational complexity. An external sensor module containing a wide-angle monocular camera and an IMU is used in this work to increase the camera's field of view (FOV).

Monocular Camera

The monocular camera can acquire a 640 × 480-pixel picture stream at 30 frames per second, and the IMU can output linear acceleration as well as angular velocity at 250 frames per second. No GPU or other acceleration methods to speed up motion tracking were used to test the efficiency of the proposed system. The cumulative processing time from feature extraction in the front end to pose optimization in the back end for each incoming frame is collected to check the processing efficiency of our visual-based tracking in smartphones. The average mobile motion tracking efficiency can achieve near-real-time accuracy. The latency trend is evident because the new filtered pose for phone AR/VR depends strongly on the prior ones.

Key Problem

As a result, a key problem for mobile AR/VR is how to perform real-time motion tracking while automatically balancing jitter and latency in various situations. The frame rate of incoming photos and IMU measurements is constant with the existing monocular camera and inertial sensor, resulting in a constant time interval between adjacent arriving poses from the visual-inertial fusion. As a result, the position changes of neighboring postures are used to differentiate between various motion circumstances in real time.

The following extensive analyses of the proposed segmented strategies are given to further explain the proposed adaptive filter system:

- Jitter filtering: So when a mobile AR/VR device is nearly stationary or runs gradually, the transition among adjacent poses can be almost neglected. As a result, the jitter phenomenon dominates in this case, whereas the latency phenomenon for mobile AR/VR users can be ignored. Such a stage is referred to as jitter-filtering in this book. At the same time, the real-time distances among arrival poses are currently small enough.

- Moderation filtering: During the work with a moderate distance pith, this stage is known as moderation filtering when the motion situation of the mobile AR/VR system is under moderate motion circumstances.

- Latency filtering: Whenever the mobile AR/VR system is subjected to rapid motion, a difference among adjacent arriving poses is dramatic. When the pose does not arrive on time, the consumer will note the latency. Therefore, in this situation for mobile AR/VR, the latency phenomenon dominates, while the jitter phenomenon can be overlooked in a fast-moving situation. Latency filtering is the term for this point.

The normalized distance among adjacent postures can be used to feed the proposed adaptive filter system, as per the preceding explanations. Thus, to solve various motion situations, the appropriate filter phase is decided. To efficiently solve the jitter and latency phenomena, quadratic functions are used in the jitter and latency stages to smooth out extreme motion conditions. Furthermore, a linear function is known as moderation filtering to bridge the jitter filtering and latency filtering stages on mobile terminals to reduce computing complexity. These segmented frameworks aim to estimate an ideal dynamic system, resulting in a simple and suboptimal solution for mobile AR/VR jitter and latency. Therefore, an adaptive filter mechanism can manage the jitter and latency for real-time motion. A qualitative experiment is conducted to test the efficiency of the proposed real-time motion tracking for mobile AR/VR. And tracking based on the actual motion scenarios for the mobile AR/VR to check device uncertainty. The visual-inerstial fusion approach can easily provide a high-frequency arriving pose with the aid of IMU, although it is prone to drift due to the combined error of IMU between the two visual frames in mobile.

Proposed Adaptive Visual-Inertial Approach

The proposed adaptive visual-inertial approach has several advantages. Furthermore, tracking stability can be enhanced when suffering from motion blur or poor texture, as per credible pose estimate by IMU within a brief period. A quantitative experiment is conducted to further validate the proposed procedure. The ground truth for the proposed approach is the trajectory obtained from the typical target pattern, which is known to have high accuracy. The smartphone AR is prone to collapsing based solely on visual-based motion tracking due to the incredible blurred picture. Even so, the tracking loss phenomena caused by fast motion blur can be alleviated using the proposed sensor fusion–dependent tracking method.

VR helps the user to communicate with the virtual world in a variety of ways. As a result, real-time monitoring of the user's postures and behaviors is crucial for a VR device. Furthermore, the frame rate for motion tracking in VR is higher than that of AR. Alternatively, the consumers will become ill as a result of the latency phenomenon. A smooth 6-DoF motion tracking for cellular VR could be accomplished in real time using the proposed adaptive visual-inertial fusion process. The 6-DoF motion of the user can be observed in real time using the proposed multi-sensor device installed on the user's head. As a result, when the user walks independently in the real world, the virtual scene's focus will adjust to match the real 6-DoF motion tracking.

Real-Time Motion Tracking

Real-time motion tracking is a critical issue for any AR/VR device, so there are a variety of ways to achieve this performance. In marker-based motion tracking, the device must first detect and recognize the marker before calculating the observer's relative pose. Even so, the marker must be placed on or near the item of concern ahead of time, and it is not always possible to do so in some cases. Furthermore, the marker must stay noticeable throughout the mobile AR/VR operation, as tracking is more likely to be corrupt if the marker is not visible. Correspondingly, another popular motion tracking system for mobile AR/VR is the model-based method. This tracking method uses a prior model of the environment to be tracked. Usually, this prior knowledge consists of 3D models or 2D templates of the real scene.

Summary

This work presented a real-time motion tracking strategy for smartphone AR/VR that is more effective than conventional visual-based marker-less tracking approaches. A monocular visual-inertial fusion is developed in the document that could effectively boost the tracking robustness and enhance frame rate with the aid of an inertial sensor, given the real-time and robust posture arriving for mobile AR/VR. Moreover, an adaptive filter system is proposed to mitigate the jitter phenomena in heterogeneous sensor fusion that can change the filter weight as per various motion circumstances, resulting in real-time and smooth motion monitoring for both technologies. Eventually, experiments are done in various AR/VR scenarios, and the outcomes indicate that the proposed approach is both robust and accurate. A segmented adaptive framework is presented in this article for a simplifying calculation, and a suboptimal output for real-time motion tracking for smartphone AR/VR is obtained. Even so, unstable transitions occur at the segmented point in tracking output, so future work will focus on a more continuous filtering system for visual-inertial fusion.

CHAPTER 7

Augmented Reality Using ARKit and OpenCV

ARKit has been one of Apple's most popular iOS 11 functionality. Many more innovative augmented reality applications are being developed daily. In this project we will focus on setting up your first Augmented Reality projects using Apple's ARKit and implementing it in Unity.

Why Do You Use OpenCV instead of Core ML?
Multiple Platforms Are Supported

Although Core ML could be the best option for an iOS 11-only iPhone app, whenever you want backward compatibility or would like to support multiple platforms, you will have to instead build a custom approach for each platform or use OpenCV.

Machine Learning isn't right for every issue. Although Apple offers a couple of free open source models for items like object as well as scene detection, the field of computer vision is far bigger than just machine learning, and OpenCV is the most convenient way to get access to these resources.

© Ahmed Fathi Bekhit 2022
A. F. Bekhit, *Computer Vision and Augmented Reality in iOS*,
https://doi.org/10.1007/978-1-4842-7462-0_7

ARKit and OpenCV Integration

Via a delegate call, ARSession allows direct access to the current frame data.

```
- (void)session:(ARSession *)session didUpdateFrame:(ARFrame *)frame;
```

When a new frame becomes visible, this function is invoked. We can get a CVPixelBufferRef of the raw data via a frame from here. Although the data in the frame is given in planar YCbCr format, we only require the grayscale version for our purposes. We miss the conversion stage and just catch the Y frame as we know it's a YUV format.

This was how we went about doing it:

```
cv::Mat mat;

CVPixelBufferLockBaseAddress(buffer, 0);

//Get only the data from the plane we're interested in

void *address = CVPixelBufferGetBaseAddressOfPlane(buffer, 0);

int bufferWidth = (int)CVPixelBufferGetWidthOfPlane(buffer, 0);

int bufferHeight = (int)CVPixelBufferGetHeightOfPlane(buffer, 0);

int bytePerRow = (int)CVPixelBufferGetBytesPerRowOfPlane(buffer, 0);

mat = cv::Mat(bufferHeight, bufferWidth, CV_8UC1, address,
bytePerRow).clone();

//Rotate the frame we receive

cv::Mat rotated;

cv::transpose(mat, rotated);

cv::flip(rotated, rotated,1);
//Do what we want with the frame
//detect faces, track objects ect.

CVPixelBufferUnlockBaseAddress(buffer, 0);
```

We only need the Y frame, which is held in the first place, as previously mentioned.

To do so, we use the `CVPixelBufferGetXOfPlane` techniques with a plane index of 0 instead of the standard `CVPixelBufferGet` methods.

Eventually, since the frame we obtain is in landscape mode, all we have to do is rotate it before moving it on to any OpenCV magic we have.

The logic is being reused.

If you're making an Augmented Reality app that also supports iOS 10, you can use the preceding approach by changing the format of your AVCaptureVideoDataOutput to fit ARKit

```
_captureOutputVideo.videoSettings = @{ (NSString
*)kCVPixelBufferPixelFormatTypeKey :
@(kCVPixelFormatType_420YpCbCr8BiPlanarVideoRange) };
```

and using the SampleBufferRef to get the same CVPixelBufferRef.

```
CVImageBufferRef imageBuffer =
CMSampleBufferGetImageBuffer(sampleBuffer);
```

To Sum Up

Although iOS 11 (and beyond) install base has been increasing, a typical augmented reality application can not solely integrate the tools included in Apple's latest update. However, by integrating the frame data we get from ARKit with OpenCV, we'll be able to build seemingly convincing interactions because they're truly augmenting truth using both low-level implementation from OpenCV and ARKit's convenience methods and APIs. Interactions can be anything from body tracking to depth analysis (Figure 7-1).

Figure 7-1. *Body Tracking with ARKit in iOS*

Prerequisite

We require a Mac computer to develop our programs and an iOS device to run them because we are building for the Apple ecosystem.

Hardware

A macOS PC that is compatible with macOS Catalina is required in terms of hardware. The strong Apple A12 Bionic CPUs are also required for body monitoring programs to function properly. The following Mac computers and iOS devices are eligible for this promotion:

Computers	Mobile devices
12-inch MacBook	iPhone XS
MacBook Air, 2012 and later	iPhone XS Max
MacBook Pro, 2012 and later	iPhone XR
Mac mini, 2012 and later	iPad Pro 11-inch
iMac, 2012 and later	iPad Pro 12.9-inch
iMac Pro	
Mac Pro, 2013 and later	

Figure 7-2. *Mac Computers and iOS Devices Eligible for This Promotion*

Software

You'll need to install the following applications on your Mac to run the demos:

- Unity3D 2019.1.5f1 with iOS build target
- MacOS Catalina 10.15 (beta)
- Xcode 11 (beta)

iOS 13 (beta) or iPadOS 13 should be installed on your device (beta).

As you'll see, the majority of the program is still in beta at the time of writing. Please remember that the devices may become sluggish or unreliable, so take extra precautions to avoid losing important data.

Body Tracking Step by Step

Let's get started with the ARKit magic. Launch Unity3D 2019.1 on your computer and start a new project (Figure 7-3).

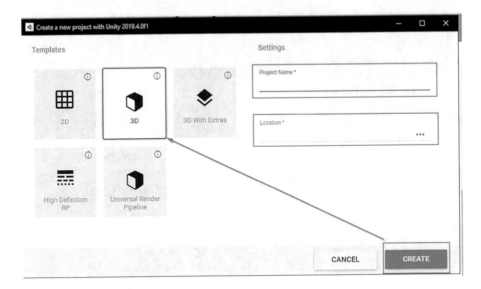

Figure 7-3. *Unity3D 2019*

Step 1: Set Up the Primary Scenario

Unity3D will begin by creating a blank scene. We must first import the necessary dependencies before adding any visual elements or writing any code. The ARKit toolkit includes skeleton-tracking capability. As a consequence, the ARKit and ARFoundation dependency packages must be imported. Make a new scene using an AR Session and an AR Session Origin object. These objects control the iOS camera while also delivering a plethora of ARKit features.

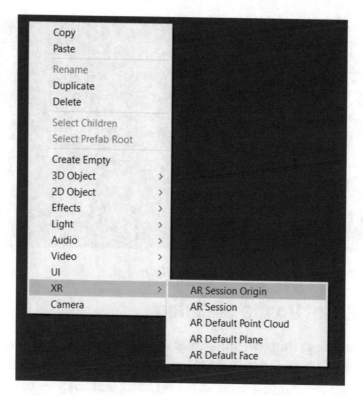

Figure 7-4. Using the Application

Furthermore, create a new C# script and attach it to an empty game object called Human Body Tracking (HumanBodyTracking.cs).

It should be like

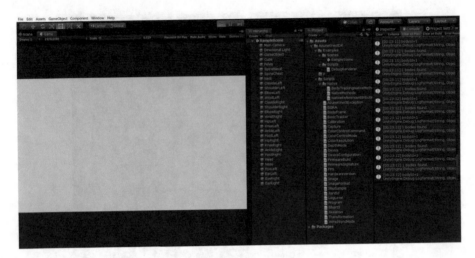

Figure 7-5. *Front End of the Application*

Step 2: Set Up the Skeleton

We can now begin implementing interactivity that the visual pieces are in place. Add a reference to the ARHumanBodyManager class to the HumanBodyTracking.cs script. The main script that analyzes camera data to detect human bodies is ARHumanBodyManager.

```
[SerializeField] private ARHumanBodyManager humanBodyManager;
```

We will use some simple Unity3D spheres to represent the joints. Each sphere would represent a different type of joint. To modify the joint data frame by frame, add a C# Dictionary class.

```
private Dictionary<JointIndices3D, Transform> bodyJoints;
```

Lastly, add references to the skeleton's user interface pieces. A sphere object will be used for the joints, and a line object will be used for the bones.

```
[SerializeField] private GameObject jointPrefab;
[SerializeField] private GameObject lineRendererPrefab;

private LineRenderer[] lineRenderers;
private Transform[][] lineRendererTransforms;
```

Step 3: Locate the Followed Bodies

It's the most crucial section of the guide! Body tracking has never been easier or more available, thanks to ARKit. Everything you have to do is subscribe to the "humanBodiesChanged" event using the ARHumanBodyManager object.

```
private void OnEnable()
{
    humanBodyManager.humanBodiesChanged += OnHumanBodiesChanged;
}

private void OnDisable()
{
    humanBodyManager.humanBodiesChanged -= OnHumanBodiesChanged;
}
```

The magic happens in the event handler. The event arguments include information on the tracked bodies. Here's how you get the bodies:

```
private void OnHumanBodiesChanged(ARHumanBodiesChangedEventArgs eventArgs)
{
    foreach (ARHumanBody humanBody in eventArgs.added)
    {
        UpdateBody(humanBody);
    }

    foreach (ARHumanBody humanBody in eventArgs.updated)
    {
        UpdateBody(humanBody);
    }
}
```

Isn't it a piece of cake? Now, let's put it all together and show the skeleton in the Unity user interface that we built in the prior iterations. Notice that ARKit only allows one tracked body as of this writing.

Step 4: Show the Skeleton

The lines of code that follow update the joint positions in the camera space. The spheres and lines are overlaid on top of the camera feed from the iOS device.

```
private void UpdateBody(ARHumanBody arBody)
{
    if (jointPrefab == null) return;
    if (arBody == null) return;
    if (arBody.transform == null) return;

    InitializeObjects(arBody.transform);

    NativeArray<XRHumanBodyJoint> joints = arBody.joints;

    foreach (KeyValuePair<JointIndices3D, Transform> item in bodyJoints)
    {
        UpdateJointTransform(item.Value, joints[(int)item.Key]);
    }

    for (int i = 0; i < lineRenderers.Length; i++)
    {
        lineRenderers[i].SetPositions(lineRendererTransforms[i]);
    }
}
```

Apple supports 92 different types of joints (indices). But not many of these types of joints are tracked! The placements of their adjoining joints are used to infer the majority of them. I've chosen 14 joint types for your convenience so that I can make a fair comparison with the Kinect camera.

This is how the appropriate joints are connected and the human bones are formed:

```
private void InitializeObjects(Transform arBodyT)
{
    if (bodyJoints == null)
    {
        bodyJoints = new Dictionary<JointIndices3D, Transform>
        {
            { JointIndices3D.head_joint, Instantiate(jointPrefab, arBodyT).transform },
            { JointIndices3D.neck_1_joint, Instantiate(jointPrefab, arBodyT).transform
            { JointIndices3D.left_arm_joint, Instantiate(jointPrefab, arBodyT).transfor
            { JointIndices3D.right_arm_joint, Instantiate(jointPrefab, arBodyT).transfc
            { JointIndices3D.left_forearm_joint, Instantiate(jointPrefab, arBodyT).tran
            { JointIndices3D.right_forearm_joint, Instantiate(jointPrefab, arBodyT).tra
            { JointIndices3D.left_hand_joint, Instantiate(jointPrefab, arBodyT).transfc
            { JointIndices3D.right_hand_joint, Instantiate(jointPrefab, arBodyT).transf
            { JointIndices3D.left_upLeg_joint, Instantiate(jointPrefab, arBodyT).transf
            { JointIndices3D.right_upLeg_joint, Instantiate(jointPrefab, arBodyT).trans
            { JointIndices3D.left_leg_joint, Instantiate(jointPrefab, arBodyT).transfor
            { JointIndices3D.right_leg_joint, Instantiate(jointPrefab, arBodyT).transfc
            { JointIndices3D.left_foot_joint, Instantiate(jointPrefab, arBodyT).transfc
            { JointIndices3D.right_foot_joint, Instantiate(jointPrefab, arBodyT).transf
        };

        lineRenderers = new LineRenderer[]
        {
            Instantiate(lineRendererPrefab).GetComponent<LineRenderer>(), // head neck
            Instantiate(lineRendererPrefab).GetComponent<LineRenderer>(), // upper
            Instantiate(lineRendererPrefab).GetComponent<LineRenderer>(), // lower
            Instantiate(lineRendererPrefab).GetComponent<LineRenderer>(), // right
            Instantiate(lineRendererPrefab).GetComponent<LineRenderer>() // left
        };


        lineRendererTransforms = new Transform[][]
        {
            new Transform[] { bodyJoints[JointIndices3D.head_joint], bodyJoints[JointIn
            new Transform[] { bodyJoints[JointIndices3D.right_hand_joint], bodyJoints[J
            new Transform[] { bodyJoints[JointIndices3D.right_foot_joint], bodyJoints[J
            new Transform[] { bodyJoints[JointIndices3D.right_arm_joint], bodyJoints[Jc
            new Transform[] { bodyJoints[JointIndices3D.left_arm_joint], bodyJoints[Joi
        };

        for (int i = 0; i < lineRenderers.Length; i++)
        {
            lineRenderers[i].positionCount = lineRendererTransforms[i].Length;
        }
    }
}
```

The position and rotation of the joints in 3D space are provided by ARKit! That's how you update the sphere's scale, location, and rotation in 2D screen space:

```
private void UpdateJointTransform(Transform jointT, XRHumanBodyJoint bodyJoint)
{
    jointT.localScale = bodyJoint.anchorScale;
    jointT.localRotation = bodyJoint.anchorPose.rotation;
    jointT.localPosition = bodyJoint.anchorPose.position;
}
```

That's it! Let's build and test our app on a real iOS device!

Step 5: Create and Deploy

Eventually, we must construct and test the project on a real device. We can't test our code on macOS because ARKit is only available on iOS and iPadOS. Select File ➤ Build Settings in Unity. Click the Build button after selecting the iOS build target. You must choose a place for the produced project to be saved. Patiently wait till Unity's build process is completed. An Xcode project will be created by Unity (.xcodeproj). Using Xcode 11 beta, open the project. You'll get an error and your project won't run properly if you use an older version of Xcode. Give your iOS development credentials, connect your iOS 13 device, and then click the Run button once the project has been launched. The project will be deployed to the device in this manner.

When you're done, point the camera toward a person to see the 3D overlay appear on top of the tracked body!

Face Tracking in ARKit 3

Figure 7-6. *Face Tracking in ARKit 3*

User Level: Basic

Augmented Reality has provided us with the ability to develop interactive and exciting opportunities for mobile technology users since its introduction to the industry. AR can save our time in a variety of ways, including checking out how our ideal sofa will look in our apartment, determining if the chosen paint color would suit the interior, and even instantly trying on new makeup.

Face tracking is a strong feature of ARKit 3 on iPhone X and newer. We can quickly create applications for trying on jewelry, lipstick, or glasses with the right components. We'll concentrate on the last choice in this example: creating an AR app for trying on glasses with a simple frame color shift.

Setup and Specifications for ARKit 3

Since the A11 Bionic chip introduced in the iPhone X is needed for AR face tracking with ARKit 3, we'll need this system or one that's newer to make our example work. We'll need Unity 2019.1 or later for our project to take advantage of all of ARKit 3's functionality, such as multiple-face tracking. We'll need to install the required ARKit packages after we've built our project. Since ARKit for Unity has been included in the ARFoundation bundle since July 2019, we'll need to open the Package Manager from the Window menu and install the following packages:

1. ARFoundation

2. AR Subsystems

3. AR Face Tracking for all the required face tracking scripts

4. XR Legacy Input Helpers for the Tracked Pose Driver script

It's a great idea to move the project to the iOS platform and set the player configuration after the installation. Set the Target minimum iOS Version to 11.0 in the Player Settings window, as ARKit 3.0 needs a minimum SDK version of 11.0.

Choose ARM64 from the Architecture dropdown in the same window, as ARKit only supports 64-bit devices. You'll also need to specify the Camera Usage Description, which is the script that will appear when the app requests approval to use the system camera. You can change the text to whatever you want, such as "ARKit 3 Face Detection."

Session Objects in Augmented Reality

We can begin creating the requisite AR Session objects once the project has been properly set up. Initially, we make an ARSession GameObject in our scene and add two scripts to it: an AR Session script and an AR Input Manager script.

Then, with an AR Session Origin script and an AR Face Manager, we create an AR Session Origin object. Since ARKit seldom uses the device's frontal camera – it's only used in face tracking/identification scenarios –

the Face Manager script is critical. There's an empty field for a Camera script in the AR Session Origin.

Let us just place the Main Camera object inside the AR Session Origin object and then reference it in the AR Session Origin script. Three scripts will be required:

- Pose Driver with Tracking (in the Tracked Pose Driver, change the Pose Source to Color Camera and enable Use Relative Transform)

- AR Camera History

- AR Camera Manager

Have you found how there's an empty field for a Face Prefab in the AR Face Manager in the AR Session Origin script? That's the prefab we'll use to imagine our AR Face–based glasses.

Prefab AR Glasses

We will need to make a new GameObject, which we named GlassesPrefab. The very first thing we need to do with our prefab is attach two components to it. The first is an ARFace variable, which will provide us with face point data that has been identified. The second is ARGlassesController, a script that will be in charge of positioning the glasses based on data updated by ARFace.

Figure 7-7. *ARFace Application*

After that, we'll need to build a GameObject within the prefab that will be attached to our glasses mesh, which we'll manipulate using the ARGlassesController. The prefab's final form should resemble that shown in the preceding image. The manipulated mesh must be saved as a child object inside our prefab. The ARFaceManager controls the location of the prefab, and the ARFace vertices are local points for features related to the detected face.

ARGlassesController Class

```
using UnityEngine;
using UnityEngine.XR.ARFoundation;
using UnityEngine.XR.ARSubsystems;

[RequireComponent(typeof(ARFace))]
public class ARGlassesController : MonoBehaviour
{
        [field: SerializeField]
        public static ARGlassesController Instance { get; private set; }

        [field: SerializeField]
        public Transform ModelTransform { get; private set; }

        [field: SerializeField]
        public Material FrameMaterial { get; private set; }

        private ARFace ARFaceComponent { get; set; }

        private const string MATERIAL_COLOR_SETTING_NAME = "_Color";
        private const int AR_GLASSES_PLACEMENT_VERTICE_INDEX = 16;

        public void ChangeFrameColor (Color color)
        {
                if (FrameMaterial != null)
                {
                        FrameMaterial.SetColor(MATERIAL_COLOR_SETTING_NAME, color)
                }
        }

        protected virtual void Awake ()
        {
                if (Instance == null)
                {
                        Instance = this;
                }
```

```
            ARFaceComponent = GetComponent();
    }

    protected virtual void OnDestroy ()
    {
            Instance = null;
    }

    protected virtual void OnEnable ()
    {
            ARFaceComponent.updated += TryToUpdateModelStatus;
            ARSession.stateChanged += TryToUpdateModelStatus;
            TryToUpdateModelStatus();
    }

    protected virtual void OnDisable ()
    {
            ARFaceComponent.updated -= TryToUpdateModelStatus;
            ARSession.stateChanged -= TryToUpdateModelStatus;
    }

    private void TryToUpdateModelStatus (ARFaceUpdatedEventArgs eventArgs)
    {
            TryToUpdateModelStatus();
    }

    private void TryToUpdateModelStatus (ARSessionStateChangedEventArgs eventArg
    {
            TryToUpdateModelStatus();
    }
```

```
protected virtual void OnDisable ()
{
        ARFaceComponent.updated -= TryToUpdateModelStatus;
        ARSession.stateChanged -= TryToUpdateModelStatus;
}

private void TryToUpdateModelStatus (ARFaceUpdatedEventArgs eventArgs)
{
        TryToUpdateModelStatus();
}

private void TryToUpdateModelStatus (ARSessionStateChangedEventArgs eventArg
{
        TryToUpdateModelStatus();
}

private void TryToUpdateModelStatus ()
{
        bool isFaceVisible = GetFaceVisibility();
        ModelTransform.gameObject.SetActive(isFaceVisible);

        if (isFaceVisible == true)
        {
                ModelTransform.localPosition = ARFaceComponent.vertices[AR_C
        }
}

private bool GetFaceVisibility()
{
        return enabled == true && ARFaceComponent.trackingState != Tracking$
}
```

ARFace Data and Face Detection in ARKit 3

The procedure is straightforward: when the ARFaceManager detects a face, it sends new ARFace data. Since our controller is linked to ARFace's updated case, the script updates the location of the glasses whenever a new set of face point coordinates is detected.

The vertex array indexes often apply to the same characteristic points on a human's face; the only thing that varies based on a person's facial characteristics is the overall location and face mesh. We aligned our glasses to vertex index 16, yielding the following outcome.

Select Color

Color Selector

We like to adjust the color of the frames using a ColorController script connected to buttons in a simple UI, so we made ARGlassesController a singleton so that the ColorController can access it whenever it's accessible on the scene.

```
using UnityEngine;

public class ColorController : MonoBehaviour
{
    [field: SerializeField]
    public Color Color { get; private set; }

        public void SetFrameColor()
        {
                if (ARGlassesController.Instance != null)
                {
                        ARGlassesController.Instance.ChangeFrameColor(Color);
                }
        }
}
```

The SetFrameColor function is linked to the Click event of each color button on the scene, allowing us to change the frame color to the one specified in the controller whenever we click a button.

Summary

The preceding instructions covered are for an Augmented Reality face tracking app. This is just one instance of many possible applications in Augmented Reality and ARKit. The ARKit face tracking APIs can be used to build rather more complicated applications, not just for fashion and cosmetics but also for industrial and enterprise applications, such as, employee identification and user authentication. Apple today provides us with sophisticated and versatile tools that could empower thousands of applications. Given a future where companies invest more into Augmented Reality hardware and software, we are thrilled to see how the technology evolves in the near future and what Apple will be offering in both hardware and software in the near future.

Index

A

Adaptive visual-inertial approach, 128
AlexNet, 37, 40
ARKit, 131, 142, 144
ARKit 3
    ARFace Data/face detection, 149
    face tracking, 143
    setup/specifications, 143, 144
    user level, 143
Artificial Intelligence (AI), 11, 20, 32–34
Artificial Neural Networks (ANNs), 13, 15, 17, 20
Augmented Reality (AR)
    aerial robotics, 27
    ARFace Data/face detection, 149
    ARGlassesController, 145
    AR Session Origin script, 144
    camera's live visual data, 22, 23
    color selector, 151, 152
    concepts, 22
    definition, 17, 22, 111
    devices, 18
    digital components, 23

digital objects, 17
face detection, 27, 28
face filters, 27
geolocation, 17, 18
geolocation-based, 29, 30
geolocation sensors, 24, 25
GlassesPrefab, 145, 146
IMUs, 26, 27
key problem, 126, 127
landmark estimation, 27, 28
location-based, 112
Main Camera object, 145
marker, 27
Marker-Based, 17–19, 27, 28, 112
Marker-Less, 17–19, 27, 29, 112
markers, 18, 28
motion model, 26
multi-lens camera, 24
pose estimation, 19
scene reconstruction, 25, 26
scripts, 145
single-lens cameras, 23, 24
video frames, 25
videoplace, 22
vision-only techniques, 26
vision task, 25

Printed in the United States
by Baker & Taylor Publisher Services